A Love Remembered

STUART DOLLERY

ACKNOWLEDGMENTS

The first person I need to thank is my wife and my absolute rock, Lisa.

Reflecting back on the happenings within this book has made me realise what an incredible journey we have been on over the years. It wasn't until I collated all the events - the highs, and the lows - that I realised just how much we had both been through.

I could not have coped even half as much without her continual love, support and belief.

I have to mention all the support from family members, Sue and Bo, my uncles and aunts, Helen, Michael, Ian and Sal, and our friends Pete and Hayley.

I also can't forget my children Josie, Ella-Rose, and the twins Tom and Olivia (Liv), all of whom I love dearly.

DEDICATION

This book is dedicated to my mum and dad, to whom I am
eternally grateful for their continual love and support.
Never forgotten.
It is also written for all those that have had to deal with,
and are dealing with, Alzheimer's and dementia. May you
find strength in the darkness.

CONTENTS

PREFACE

Today the journey begins. The storytelling journey. It's been a long while coming. I've talked about this for such a long time, and it feels great to finally begin.

You know what they say? Starting is often the hardest part, so here goes!

So, why this book, and why me?

I'm writing this book primarily for others. For those whose lives have been affected by Alzheimer's and dementia. This includes the person themselves, and the total support network around that person, which can be far reaching.

I do also hope however, from my own standpoint, that by baring my soul there will be a level of personal catharsis.

As a Personal Trainer, one thing I always encouraged my clients to do (and my kids actually) was to share. Certainly not always the easiest thing to do, but I do believe a trouble shared is a trouble halved.

In writing about my dear mum and dad, who both dealt with Alzheimer's and dementia, respectively. I hope that you the reader can learn and understand from mine and their experiences, and hopefully find some solace.

Whilst they both had quite different personal journeys, this book looks at how I dealt with them on a day-to-day basis; my feelings and emotions, and the practical mechanisms that helped to keep me (semi) sane.

This book explores the battle of what I called the 'real Mum' versus the 'Alzheimer's Mum', how her condition manifested itself, and what we had to do to manage it the best we could.

I also talk about my dad's general development of dementia, my relationship with him, and how effectively I walked a tightrope of coerciveness, role reversal, and direct communication.

I refer to a 'rollercoaster' many times throughout the book because that's exactly how it felt. An unpredictable ride of highs and lows, and everything in between, all whilst my wife, Lisa, and I juggled our own self-employed businesses, and kept our four kids entertained and fed!

I am certainly no expert on Alzheimer's or dementia, I just wanted to share our story in an effort to help others. Hopefully, you will sense the realness, and maybe even the rawness as you delve further into the book.

This book is very different from my last, not technical or particularly academic. No, it's a record of all my emotions and feelings, written and reflected upon, and a sharing of all my collective experiences using all of my senses.

If this book helps you to learn and understand the Alzheimer's and dementia journey a little better, gets you to think ahead for the logistics involved, assists in the firefighting, or provides you with some skills to help deal with it, then I feel I've done my job.

Whilst I can honestly say it was a very tough experience to go through personally, I think you learn so much about yourself and it makes you stronger.

I'm a firm believer that out of something inherently bad can come something good, even if it's a tough life lesson.

I've always learnt more from challenging experiences and grown as a consequence, something you don't always realise until you take time to reflect.

I hope that by reading my book you can understand that, despite the rocky road, you can stay strong, remember the better times, and learn lots about yourself in the process.

Believe that you will become a better version of

yourself by supporting those you love and care for most through one of the cruellest conditions.

CHAPTER ONE
MUM, DAD AND ME

If you haven't read the preface, then this first chapter provides the back story to what happened to my parents and I, prior to any inkling that we might be dealing with Alzheimer's or dementia. It's my hope this will give you an understanding of what life was like for us all before the diagnosis, and give an insight into them as people.

My mum, Diana, affectionally knowing as Di by most, was born in Churt, Surrey, on 30th October 1943, the daughter of Thomas Ivan Murgatroyd and Phyllis Murgatroyd (nee Hatch).

Thomas, a former Royal marine, joined two spinsters at Pine House and became their chauffeur, and gardener. Phyllis was their housekeeper and cook.

Diana was the eldest, and she had two brothers Michael

and then Ian, the youngest.

They lived in Pine House cottage, which was built for them, beside the big house, by the spinsters, so they could live close to work.

Looking back on it, my nan and grandad actually thought that the spinsters were lovers, but sadly it was at a time where they hadn't felt they could let it be widely known. I'd like to think things have moved on since then, but who knows? Until recently I had believed there had been more acceptance on gay relationships and things had progressed, but recently however my youngest Liv and her girlfriend had drinks thrown over them, just for holding hands, walking through town.

Mum went to school at Beacon Hill Primary and then onto Woolmer Hill Secondary until the age of 16. She left school to work at a grocery store, Burgesses Delicatessen, in the parade, Hindhead. I seem to remember she would have liked to have gone onto further education, but I believe Thomas had other ideas. I think he was quite persuasive that she must get a job.

As luck would have it, my dad was living in accommodation in the same row of shops and would visit the shop where Mum worked often. She caught his eye as the new shop assistant, and I'm not too sure if he used any good one liners, but they arranged a date, and the rest is history as they say. I'm certainly glad it worked out!

My dad, christened Colin Harry George Dollery, was born at the Parade, Hindhead, Surrey. Fathered by George Dollery and mother Elizabeth, they also had Margaret.

Sadly Elizabeth, or Betty as she was known, died of Tuberculosis when Dad was just 7 years old.

George remarried and they had Derek. Louise, Dad's stepmum, had been previously married, but unfortunately her husband died as a pilot in World War Two. They had a daughter together, Sonia.

It wasn't until I asked my Aunt Margaret about her childhood, I realised that before George remarrying, my dad had been sent away to live with Granny Dollery, and Margaret to Emsworth to another relative.

Although Dad never really explained himself, I sensed that he found growing up hard being separated from his sister, losing his mother so young (she was only 31), and then having a new stepmum.

Dad went to Godalming Grammar School prior to going into the RAF. I know he really wanted to go onto further education, but I don't think he had the right financial support or the encouragement at that time.

My parents married locally in Churt, at the same church my Nanny Phyllis and Grandad Tom had, and then afterwards they had the function at Pine House. The spinsters' house was perfect for functions as it had a huge music room and beautiful sweeping lawns, with manicured gardens. They held some quite high-brow concerts there apparently, with one spinster being a concert pianist in her own right.

The photos of the day were stunning, with one of them, of the bridesmaids, winning a local photography competition.

Afterwards, Mum travelled extensively with Dad, as he moved around with the Royal Air Force, covering places like Ely, Holton, and Witney, to name a few.

He ended up being in the air force for 18 years!

Mum and Dad desperately wanted children, and after many years trying and a few hiccups along the way, they finally had me. I can even remember Mum telling me that she'd get Dad home for `lunch' and then her doing post coital handstands to increase the chances!

Sadly, for them, I was their only child, not for the want of trying.

When my father left the RAF, he went into business with my Uncle Michael and set up D & M Services -

Dollery and Murgatroyd Services, doing general building work, extensions and suchlike. Michael was a qualified bricklayer and my Dad did electrics and plumbing, amongst other things.

Then my uncle Ian joined as a carpenter and my Grandad as painter and decorator - it was definitely a family affair. After a number of successful years my dad decided to broaden his horizons and left D & M for pastures new.

Dad was naturally a hands on gentleman, and I use that term because he was very much a 'gentle man.' He was naturally intelligent and a great problem solver. He had an engineering mind, so was naturally inquisitive and loved nothing more than applying logic to any situation. This was a point he proved when he scored very highly on the MENSA IQ test which he took in London. We already knew that though!

I remember how he loved to read, and was always learning. His toilet reading list, alongside aircraft books, would be things like Stephen Hawking and topics like Quantum Physics - not your usual bathroom reading material!

He then started work for Sperry Gyroscope, focusing on underwater mining systems and testing.

Whilst he was there, my mum worked in Liss, Hampshire, in a fruit and vegetable shop that was also a florists. She learnt how to apply her artistic flair by making flower arrangements, bouquets and wiring elaborate shapes and names, like you sometimes see at funerals and special events.

I remember her talking about the travellers coming in with big wads of cash, when one of their own had passed. They really went to town with a lot of quite complex flower arrangements, which meant her working overtime to get them all done.

I remember her being a 'worrier', a fact highlighted when, on looking concerned she exclaimed, "I'm worried, because I have nothing to worry about!"

It is this very fact that makes me ponder on my mum's illness. Was her seemingly inherent worrying a factor in her demise? I can't imagine it helped.

From some of my other reading, it appears that your own 'thinking' can have a huge impact on your physical, mental and overall physiology, so perhaps?

It seems incredulous that your own thinking can change you on so many levels, but I am a firm believer in, you are what you think. My mum was definitely an over thinker, and it wasn't always positive thoughts that dominated.

Sperry Gyroscope got taken over by British Aerospace Engineering (BAE) and that took us all to lots of different places in the UK - Scotland, Farnborough, Weymouth and latterly Bristol.

In Scotland, Dad worked on projects like Polaris missiles, and other secret or classified projects. In fact, it wasn't until I cleared out their house that I released how high level some of these were. I found numerous signed and sealed papers, that if stopped would allow safe passage through customs and security.

Dad didn't really talk about his work, not because he didn't want to, but mainly because he wasn't allowed to!

Scotland for the whole family was quite a big move, but I sensed it was a happy one. My Dad, for one, embraced the outdoor life, cycling to and from work, and enjoying sailing on the loch in his Graduate dinghy. In all weathers I hasten to add, including a gale six storm, where the lifeboat was called out by a worried observer (no, not my mum surprisingly, who was luckily oblivious at the time).

My mum quickly embraced Scottish life and with each day was becoming less of a Sasanach!

I also enjoyed Scotland very much and embraced the outdoor life.

Mum was definitely a people person - she needed to be

around others and she was a very loyal, loving person. She quickly became involved in the community, and made many friends.

Whilst she was outgoing, and very much a people-centred person, she did however sometimes lack confidence, and I think it stemmed from her low self-esteem. She was quite good at covering that up though, even during the occasional bouts of depression she suffered.

It was lovely looking back at all the photos when we cleared their house, and it reminded me just what fun and naughtiness she brought. Wonderful photos of her proper 'LOL-ing' before we even knew what that meant!

Sadly, I'd almost forgotten what I called the 'real' Mum traits, as the Alzheimer's stripped away the core of her personality.

After Scotland, we moved down to Hampshire - Whitehill to be precise - near Bordon. It was an army town, with barracks nearby, but Dad's commute was about an hour by car - a bit far for him to cycle as he had in Scotland!

He had a Fiat 126, which had a tiny 652cc engine, which looking back, was pretty much the smart car of its day!

It reminded me of when I'd been fishing and asked him

to pick me up. Through crossed wires, he thought I was solo, but I actually had two friends, plus all our tackle in tow. I can remember how he fell about laughing when he saw us. Amazingly, we all fitted in, bags, kit, and all the rods poking out of the sunroof!

I went from secondary school in Scotland in year two, straight into year four, due to the different school systems. Despite the big changes, I settled well into Mill Chase school. I was made head boy in my last year, so I must have made a good impression.

I think both Mum and Dad were happier being back in an area they knew well, and being much closer to all our relatives. Mum was especially close to my nan and grandad, and we all did lots with them. What was left of Dad's family were close by, but he didn't see them so much.

We lived in this area for several years, and I went to Alton sixth form, a short bus ride away. After passing my driving test, it was a much quicker journey, in my very first car!

I had a classic mini that I used to bomb around in, with a tape cassette and boxed speakers that used to blare out. My mum always said she could hear me coming long before I arrived!

Dad was asked to transfer his work to Weymouth, full-time. He moved down before Mum and I, and he settled initially in a seafront flat, which his work put him up in. Mum and Dad then purchased their own house, which he did up in his spare time.

During this time, I was studying at West Sussex Institute of Higher Education for my BA (hons) in Sport Studies.

I think whilst Mum loved the house and the area, she found it a little harder to integrate and make friends here for some reason. She was used to moving around, but I guess some places were easier than others.

It was during this time that Dad was diagnosed with his first cancer. This was after a second opinion, as he was still not feeling right. They found a huge growth in his tummy, and even though at the time he was given just 6 weeks to live, after an operation and all the chemotherapy, he managed to pull through.

He had three different lots of cancers over his lifetime, so he was a definite survivor on that front. He ended up being invited back to Southampton Hospital to support and mentor cancer patients after this. It was a lovely way to 'give back', and to show patients with similar issues they could also recover well.

Weymouth ended up being only a few years, because not long after our move it had been decided to shut that branch of British Aerospace down. So sadly, they had to move, once again.

Dad had basically gutted the house and renewed most things; kitchen, bathrooms, etc. so I think he was disappointed, once again, to have to relocate, as he had got the house pretty much where he wanted it. They did however know the drill by now!

Whilst I was finishing my studies, they moved to Didmarton, near Tetbury in Gloucestershire, where Dad worked in the Bristol branch of BAE.

I moved back in with them for a short while after my degree, which was tougher than I thought, as whilst I loved my parents dearly, I had been independent for three years, I had got used to just doing my own thing.

I got my first 'proper' job at a Shire Inns Hotel - the Aztec Hotel, in Almondsbury, Bristol; a brand new hotel at the time.

I was a jack-of-all trades there really, but under the official title of Leisure Assistant, which meant gym instructing, fitness testing, lifeguarding, reception duties, memberships and from what I remember, lots of cleaning!

I then worked for Livingwell at another local hotel, doing much the same, but extending my C.V., by teaching aqua aerobics, which I loved.

It was however, in my next job, that something quite significant happened.

I had just accepted a new job with Livingwell, and had even put a deposit down on a flat, in what would be their flagship club in Manchester. It was better pay, and an exciting prospect. However, when I worked out my cost of living, against my income, I soon realised that I had pretty much nothing to go out with. I relinquished my contract, and looked closer to home once again.

I then managed to get a job much closer to home on the outskirts of Bristol, a relatively new club called Ambassadors Health and Fitness Club. It was an old mansion that had been converted, with two gyms, a swimming pool and function rooms, set in beautiful grounds with a long sweeping driveway. I felt instantly at home.

Little did I know it at the time, but a member there had rather taken a shine to me, and booked an assessment and programme design. That young lady was Lisa, in fact the very person I would marry, all those years later!

We hadn't known each other for that long when we moved in with each other, to be closer to where I was working. It worked out really well actually because Lisa's brother Robert was moving out, and it was only a 10 minute drive away from the gym, compared to 50 minutes from my parents'.

I had been running some exercise classes, gym instructing and had set up private one to one personal training sessions outside of the gym, visiting people's houses.

In fact, it had been a local personal trainer that inspired me to think about doing it myself. I found out, many years later, that he had in fact died at the very young age of 54, of Alzheimer's.

I then went on to work for another health club in Bristol, Viva! Health and Fitness club, as a senior instructor and then fitness and duty manager. It was an exciting prospect as it was the start of a brand-new chain, aiming for five star standards. In fact, they sold out of memberships prior to opening, a UK first.

Whilst working here I was also asked to be a visiting lecturer at the University of the West of England, on the fitness element of the psychology undergraduates course.

I think because we actively shared our knowledge and gave seminars to members, it gave us a platform to show what we knew, and I was approached by a member of their faculty staff.

It was during this time also, that Lisa and I got married in August, on probably the hottest day of 1997!

My mum, showing no signs of anything being wrong at

17

that time, was in her absolute element. She loved a good knees-up, and was so looking forward to our big day.

Lisa's parents, Sue and Bo, organised a marquee in their garden, and had their butcher friend Don do a hog roast in the evening. I have amazing memories from that day, especially how happy everyone was, and how great it was to get all the family and friends together.

Not that long after that, we had two children in close succession, Josie and Ella-Rose. We had assumed that it might take a while for Lisa to get pregnant, but how wrong were we! It was pretty much instant.

I can still hear Lisa saying, "OMG! OMG!" Whilst doing her pregnancy test!

Obviously, our life changed immeasurably for the better, with the start of our own family, with both sets of grandparents helping out where they could.

Mum and Dad by then had moved to Spider Cottage in Lower Stanton St. Quinton, near Chippenham.

It was whilst she was at Spider Cottage that Mum started to show signs that something was not quite right. Initially, it was minor things like forgetfulness or maybe repeating conversations, but then more physical factors like losing some use of her left (dominant) hand.

Dad had retired from BAE by then, and had set up his

health and safety consultancy, furthering his knowledge, and helping small businesses comply with legislation.

Even at this point we hadn't fully clocked what was happening with Mum, it was just put down to other factors; stress, depression, overall wellness decline, etc.

Little did we know at that time what was coming.

I ended up working for a fitness training organisation that trained instructors and ran courses. I did NVQ assessing and verifying, helping students to learn and get qualified within the industry. This, whilst both fascinating and exciting, unfortunately took a toll on my overall wellness.

The long working hours and driving had substantially weakened my immune system, to the point where I was suddenly rushed to hospital.

I was off work for 3 months, with a virus akin to chronic fatigue. I think it was my body telling me I couldn't carry on the way I was. My mum and dad helped Lisa and I, by covering wages lost while being on statutory sick pay.

The right time came to jump ship, when I was approached by one of the personal trainers I had actually employed before at Viva!, asking whether I wanted to set up a one to one studio with her.

Despite the fact that I was a going from safe steady

employment, to being self-employed in a brand-new business, I decided I'd love to do it, and had to take the gamble. In fact, Lisa encouraged me to. I didn't know it at the time, but it was to be one of the best decisions I'd ever made.

Whilst building my client base, I had a number of jobs to ensure that we had enough money coming in. As well as doing village hall and health club classes, I was also employed as an NHS exercise physiologist, but all that meant was that I lead the cardiac rehabilitation exercise classes at Frenchay Hospital.

I felt very honoured to help all those that had either had a heart attack or had just had a procedure. I thought back to those days where I'd be concerned if I had just one class participant that had heart issues, and yet here I was with all 50 in a class!

During these early years I was also asked to help run a G.P. Referral course at Frenchay surgery and each week did a one-hour lecture and 45 minute exercise class.

Around that time too, Lisa fell pregnant again. Poor Lisa, she suffered badly with Hyperemesis (extreme morning sickness), throughout all her pregnancies and so was in hospital again.

She rang me at work, this was how the conversation went...

LISA: Hello Stu!

ME: Hello Lis, are you ok?

LISA: Not really, as I've been so sick, but I have some news, what do you think I'm going to tell you?

And in my head, I'm thinking, well surely it can't be twins, can it?

I was silent, until Lisa said: It's twins!!

Me: OMG! OMG!

And with that poor Lisa just burst into tears. I was dumbfounded and had to let the news sink in!

We were obviously over the moon when they arrived, both safe and healthy born via Caesarian. We had a girl - christened Olivia, but prefers just Liv, and a boy named after my Grandad Thomas, who we called Tom.

Both sets of grandparents were gushing as expected, and obviously helped with the sudden doubling of our children. We felt blessed. My mum and dad were able to make up for their only child with now having four grandchildren.

So, that's most of the back story up until this point. I'm hoping you got to understand a little bit more about my family and I, and what happened prior to my mum and dad's diagnoses. I will fill you in with much more detail as the story progresses.

CHAPTER TWO
THE JOURNEY BEGINS

As I write this, I have just returned from the funeral of a lovely local lady, Daphne, who also sadly had Alzheimer's. Luckily for Rob, her partner of many years, her condition wasn't drawn out, as can sometimes be the case.

A shock indeed for all involved, but you certainly wouldn't wish any extension of this illness.

I think it's only natural to personally reflect on these occasions, but in this case even more so, as sadly, we had all been to this crematorium before.

I must admit I did get emotional. I only have to see other people get upset and I start crying. I believe I do have empathic tendencies, so it makes sense to me. Lisa and the kids always look at me when there is an emotional moment on TV for example, because they know that it sets me off!

I really felt for Rob, her husband, because he did so

much for her, and was determined to do it on his own. I could see parallels here to my mum and dad's story, albeit over less time.

Knowing what my dad did for my mum in the early days, put it all into perspective - feeding, cleaning, changing nappies, manual handling, dressing… the list was as endless as it was exhausting, both physically and mentally.

I massively respect for him for this, but I do believe there was a price to pay for his selfless behaviour.

I absolutely get it. Because my dad had exactly the same mindset - he never forgot his wedding vows – 'for better for worse'. He promised her he would take care of her at home, for as long as he could. As you will read later, that didn't quite go to plan.

I do feel, without a shadow of a doubt, that my dad's health suffered as a result of being the primary carer for my mum. He wasn't the healthiest person by default, but his own health was put on the back burner, while he focused all his efforts on my mum.

So, where do we start with the story of my beautiful mum?

I have already written some family background, so you have an inkling on her earlier life story, but I'd like to delve deeper, into when we first started to notice that something was not quite right.

And here's the thing - at what point do you start noticing that there might be an issue?

In my experience there's very much a blurred line.

I think my dad realised something was up with Mum before anyone else in the family, which makes sense, as they were living together 24/7.

On reflection, I think he was in denial. I totally get that, after all, would you want to believe what it could potentially be? The prospect was hugely frightening.

I think as we get older there is a natural decline of some of our cognitive function anyway, but it's recognising when it becomes more of a life affecting issue.

I notice even now that I easily forget names, or names of places or things, or the classic of going into a room, and trying to remember what I went in there for in the first place!

I think hormonal changes as we age influence many factors.

Pre-Alzheimer's, Mum was always losing her glasses anyway, so got them put on a chain around her neck. Prior to that she might have even had her glasses on her head and wonder where they were!

One thing I commented on earlier was what I called the 'real Mum' and the 'Alzheimer's Mum'. 'Real Mum' was obviously pre-Alzheimer's, but there was also a grey area where 'real Mum' was present as 'Alzheimer's Mum' was trying to take hold. A worrying and horrible stage for her, but more of that later.

She was truly a beautiful soul - gregarious, effervescent, bubbly with an infectious laugh, and a lovely naughty sense of humour (most people are pretty sure I inherited that from her!).

I think I might have inherited the laugh too, as when I was on a course in London, with over 800 attendees, in a breakout group somebody said, "Oh you're the guy with that laugh!"

She was always truly selfless, putting others' needs ahead of her own. If you were a friend of Di, then you had the most loyal and loving companion, who would do anything for you. She was always great fun to be around, loved family gatherings, especially where there was a huge spread of food. I think this was inherited from my lovely Nanny Phyl, who would prepare a feast fit for a king. Where the table would groan under the weight of food - think food prepared for 25, when in fact there was only 12 of us!

My Mum was definitely a 'feeder' and loved making and preparing food, and she particularly loved watching people enjoying her food.

We always used to laugh when going to my Nanny Phyl's, as she was exactly the same - she would pretty much open the door to my friends with a plate of sandwiches!

Mum was very house proud, and always kept the house spick-and-span. This included flower arrangements, both fresh and dried, scattered throughout the house. Mum loved nothing more than Christmas, and this is where the house was taken to a whole new level of decoration.

The decorations started to make an appearance as early as she would dare!

She loved spraying dried flowers gold and silver, and long garlands of local greenery were festooned down the stairs, with the obligatory baubles, and sprigs of holly on any surface she saw fit.

Mum was known to play Christmas carols in August - no joke!

I'm very pleased to say my youngest, Liv, carries this torch with pride - the film 'Elf' is watched as early as September!

In fact, thinking about it, Easter was another favourite time too. Simnel cake and Easter biscuits were made, and the freshest spring flowers were arranged. I can picture it now, her impressive arrangements with a cascade of bright yellow and white, against the backdrop of the green foliage.

I also always think of her when I see the little yellow fluffy chicks that she used to put on her cakes, usually with a few Cadbury's mini eggs for good measure.

Mum loved collecting what I would call knick-knacks or trinkets; bowls, figurines, copper pans, ornate glasses, dishes, plates, you name it. A point illustrated all too well when we cleared out the house, filling boxes and boxes with the stuff. The charity shop did rather well from our clearing, but I think that was a nice 'full circle' moment, as she was generous to a fault and would definitely have approved. Especially as she had spent many hours there, looking for a bargain or two.

She loved going to bric-a-brac and charity shops, antiques centres etc, but the 'pièce de résistance' was always the boot sales - oh my, she absolutely adored those - I can see my dad raising his eyes already!

So anyway, I digress. I think you get the picture.

I feel it is important that you understand the real Mum prior to her Alzheimer's because, there's no beating around the bush, she changed immeasurably. Sometimes it was in quite subtle ways, and other times in quite stark jumps.

From what I understand already, it appears everyone's 'journey' can be very different.

I have to admit it's difficult to pinpoint the exact starting point of her illness. Around that time, Lisa, the children, and I, lived just over an hour away from Mum and Dad's; from ours in Burnham-on-Sea, to theirs just outside Chippenham. We visited frequently, and they also came over to us. If they came over to ours, Lisa would sometimes cook a roast dinner or sometimes they would take us out, just to make things easier.

As things progressed though, albeit slowly, there was a slight withdrawal and fewer visits to us, although we didn't pick up on it at first. I'm not too sure if this was a conscious decision, or just a natural way of dealing with increasing issues.

From my perspective, before we had an inkling anything was remotely wrong, one thing that did stick in my mind, was when they came to stay to look after the children so Lisa and I could enjoy a night away. Even then, however, we didn't put two and two together.

Firstly, we had a call from Josie our eldest, who was

probably only seven at the time, that Nanny Di had shouted at her, and it had frightened her. Well, this was hugely out of character, so I can totally understand why Josie was scared. Mum adored the children, and certainly wouldn't want to hurt or upset them, on any level. She had never raised her voice to any of the children prior to this.

After the weekend, Mum casually slipped into conversation that something weird had happened to her. When she was returning from town with all the children, despite the fact that she had been to our house many times, she said she had forgotten how to get back. Afterwards we pieced together that the children, despite their young years, had helped her find her way - thank goodness!

For some reason, even though it was hugely out of character, we put it down to hormones or just her being tired or unwell.

At this point we didn't discuss anything with Dad, as we didn't think anything was particularly wrong. I do wonder if he would have played this down anyway, at this stage?

As you already know Mum was an excellent cook and loved baking, I think it helped to curb her sweet tooth, which my eldest Josie, has definitely inherited (sweets are still in top position on the Christmas list - even in her 20's)!

Mum loved to bake things for the children and bring over their favourite treats and they were always making requests. I seem to remember her rice crispy cakes made with melted toffees were a regular treat.

Around this time, Lisa asked her to make Banoffee pie, as the kids loved that, but she had made it with grapes instead of the more traditional banana.

I can remember my Nanny Phyl telling me at the time, that Mum's driving had also got bad and she had, unusually, driven up the kerb. Initially, Mum was blaming her eyesight, but whoever made the decision, it was agreed that she stop driving. That must have been very tough because some of her independence was gone.

She'd stopped writing too, which she absolutely adored. She loved putting pen to paper and was very good at keeping all her friends in the loop with her day-to-day musings. She always bought those packs of notelets with nice pictures or photos on them (generally flowers or cute animals), and would write to her many friends scattered around the globe.

In a relatively short space of time, she'd lost two of her great loves, driving AND writing. What a very cruel blow. We also noticed that she had started holding one arm up/hand across her upper body. We thought it was strange but didn't question it. In fact, she had been doing it for a while, before we fully sussed that she wasn't really using it anymore. On investigation, initially the doctors thought her issue with her arm could be the result of Arthritis, and then it was suggested that she might have even had a stroke.

We started to notice too that stairs and escalators were becoming a real challenge.

My Aunt Sal recalled that on a trip to the Mall, Mum was extremely frightened to use the escalators, so much so, they had to go a longer route to avoid them. My Aunt Helen also remembered this was a particularly hard challenge, and the stairs, especially descending, where she had literally frozen on the spot from fear of falling. Poor Mum, it must have been incredibly frightening for her.

I can remember that at a big family gathering, all of us were going down the stairs towards the beach, and it taking lots of physical support and comforting, to get through this relatively basic task. The fear was palpable. Something was happening to Mum, and it was getting harder to ignore.

Family members had noticed she was losing dexterity in her hands for everyday function, things like putting a coat or gloves on.

I recall a conversation I'd had with my Nanny Phyl, where she had been unusually emotional. Mum had been living with her to help her convalesce after a hip replacement operation.

My nan, bless her, was such a lovely person, very loving and would do anything for you, but at the same time, she kept a stiff upper lip and just soldiered on regardless. She played everything down, and was a real Trojan. We reckoned if she had a leg hanging off, it would be a 'mere inconvenience' and just a 'scratch!'

So it was a quite a surprise, when having a quiet one-to-one with her, that she started to cry, saying to me she felt something wasn't quite right with Mum. She never did explain in detail, but we too had started to consider that something wasn't 'quite right with Mum'.

My Aunt Sal recounted to me the time when she stayed with Nan during that same time period. Mum would go to make a drink and just repeatedly boil the kettle or leave drawers open. She felt that something wasn't right. Nan had said to her, that she felt Mum was, 'away with the fairies.'

Sadly a little while after that, my Nan passed away with an aneurism, very suddenly, as these things often are. It was quite a shock to those left behind, but certainly a lot better than a long drawn-out illness. I think I'd rather go that way. She was 91 when she passed and had recently enjoyed a lovely day out with both my mum and dad. The lovely cardigan she bought that day, was part of her final resting outfit.

My grandad was totally distraught at my nan's passing. He was inconsolable. They had been together since she was 14, so you can understand why.

I had never really understood grieving until that point, other than it was a necessary process. It was very painful watching my grandad go through it.

We were all very concerned for him, as Nan was his absolute rock; not that he would have ever admitted it. You just knew it, though.

I'd read stories previously about people dying from a broken heart, and that is exactly what happened, as Grandad sadly, passed away only 10 weeks later. He had given up, and he didn't want to live without my nan, so very sad.

They had been together since my nan was 14, she died aged 91, making 77 years together! So, as tough as it was, and fully understanding why he would feel that way, it didn't make it any easier for those of us left behind. We took some solace in the fact he was with her once again.

As a symbol of their love and time together, their ashes were mixed in their final resting place, at the church where they got married. Full circle.

Obviously, this was a hugely emotional time for Mum. I think she was in shock, with both parents passing in such close succession. We all were really, but Mum more so, as she was so very close to both of them.

With all the recent goings on, post funeral, Dad organised a holiday for them both, which I think was well overdue and needed. They were well-travelled, but in recent years hadn't wandered far. That's why we were a little surprised when he said they were going to Greece. Despite my worries about the logistics of it all, we felt that it would do them both good.

Looking back now I feel very sure that Dad must have realised that would be their last 'proper' holiday, so he wanted to do something extra special.

That makes me so sad, as they had done so much together over the years, he must have reflected so much on that holiday.

Despite the denial, it must have been in his thoughts how Mum was starting to act and be, and that perhaps, just maybe, he needed to instigate some action.

The next huge milestone that came up was Mum and Dad's golden wedding anniversary - 50 years, wow!

Dad started to organise a big get-together, and set about contacting their whole address book, spanning many years, and booked a function room at a local golf club.

Unbeknown to them, Lisa and I had put together a photo board, organised a balloon company to come in and decorate it all golden, and we also made a memory tree.

I'd seen the idea online, where you make a tree and get people to write their favourite memories about the person or people. I luckily managed to get a golden Christmas tree (out of season) and cut out some cards, threading them with gold ribbon. When everyone was there, I went round and explained what I'd like them to do and people steadily hung the cards on the tree.

We had some lovely memories, which in the current situation, was certainly very fitting. With all the faces from so many different eras, Mum did get a little confused as to who everyone was, and I think it threw a few people off. You could tell, sadly, that they had sussed out what was going on with her.

Looking at the photos from the night, Mum was obviously very happy, but there was a 'rabbit in headlights' look about her.

Dad asked me to give a little speech, and Lisa, Tom

and Ella did a little dance for everyone!

We made wonderful memories that day, and I hope Mum and Dad took in all that they needed - they certainly seemed to be really enjoying it!

With both of my grandparents gone and everyone rallying together to clear their house, the aunts and uncles wanted to broach the subject of Mum.

Things were starting to add up, and we could not ignore the elephant in the room.

A few concerns were mentioned to my father, from close relatives, and whilst these comments were listened too, we wondered if they were processed or just compartmentalised and lodged in a convenient storage box in his brain.

My dear dad was as stubborn as a mule, as the saying goes, in fact, if there was something more stubborn than that, Dad was it!

As much as we loved him, Dad would only do things when he wanted, which could be infuriating to say the least.

My dad was bright, (remember MENSA, right?) but I felt he didn't want to recognise that anything sinister was going on, and to be honest he didn't like being told what to do either! We refer to this as 'Dollery obstinance'-

which I'm sure my wife might say I have a touch of occasionally!

At the same time, I genuinely think my mum was frightened of not understanding what was going on mentally, but also her decline in physical function.

Looking back, this phase was where 'real Mum' was starting to battle with 'Alzheimer's mum' (despite no actual diagnosis as of yet).

It must have been frightening for her to not fully understanding why she was doing, or not doing, things, as she had before.

On reflection, it was a heart-wrenching time, and whilst I'm hugely empathic, unless you are processing this yourself, how can you really know?

The brain can do strange things at the best of times, let alone when it's under attack. So, as things were going extremely slowly in relation to getting her help, and our worries were falling on deaf ears, our concerns continued to escalate.

At a family wedding, a few family members had a quiet word with me, to express their concerns about her, and were getting forceful in saying I needed to take control and do something about it.

If Dad wouldn't, I had to.

And here's the thing. In my head of course, yes it was the right thing to do, but the reality meant being more forceful with Dad, and what felt like, over-ruling him. We had quite a traditional relationship, where he was definitely superior to me. I had to respect him, and his wishes.

So, now I'm stuck between a rock and a hard place. My mum obviously needs help, and is suffering; and my dad, who must also have been suffering in his own way, appeared to be in denial. He had to be persuaded to take action.

I totally agreed action needed to be taken, and urgently, but what was the strategy?

How was I going to ensure something was finally done?

I plucked up the courage, chose my moment, and had a hard conversation with Dad, where both Lisa and I explained our concerns for Mum, and that we thought that there was something more serious going on.

I think that, and the fact she was also getting concerned for herself (albeit in confusion), prompted some intervention, and with that some guidance from the medical community.

Looking back, I think Dad had already reasoned some of these thoughts too himself because surprisingly he was quite compliant to the idea of getting Mum further investigated. It had been a matter that had been conveniently logged away, but I think he now realised that it needed to come to the forefront and have more urgent attention. As I've already discussed, he was a man of few words, even if they were long ones (!) but the few words he did say spoke volumes.

CHAPTER THREE
THE DIAGNOSIS

After discussing Mum's issues with her GP, they conducted some tests on her brain and questioned her as best they could. She was then invited to the local hospital to discuss their findings.

The day had arrived to be informed of the diagnosis, and the mood was pensive from the off.

We walked to the main building, and I was anxious, so I can only imagine how Mum was feeling. If I could have taken any worry or pain from her, I would have done it in a flash.

Dad, Mum, Lisa and I, were ushered into a small featureless room, with a long narrow high window, five chairs (one for the specialist, and four for us), where we waited. I sat next to Dad for support and Lisa sat next to my mum, holding her hand.

I will never forget that day.

The specialist, who mistakenly thought we already knew the prognosis, said, "Well, yes, as you know Diana, the tests show that you have Alzheimer's/dementia."

Pause.

Shock.

Disbelief.

Yes of course we all thought it, but it's another thing to actually hear the words.

Mum just said, "Oh, no!" She looked visibly shaken and extremely concerned, and started crying.

Lisa and I looked at each other. We had pretty much guessed as much, but didn't like it 100% confirmed.

Dad, in only the way he could, looked composed but was obviously concerned. We listened to the specialist, but as you can imagine it was all a blur, making it difficult to take in the enormity of it all after that point.

The specialist talked about what medication might help Mum. At the time, there were three types, and they suggested she try one and see how she felt.

From the little I understood at the time, it could have helped improve her day-to-day symptoms as well as helping her reasoning and memory loss.

It was stressed though, that it didn't work for everyone, and they might have to try different treatments and dosages.

One thing in the back of my mind was that it was a late diagnosis, due to the reasons already mentioned - including, huge procrastination on our part.

I have to admit, and I guess it's only human to feel this way, but I question myself as to whether I could have been more persuasive in getting her diagnosed earlier, but I think my relationship with my dad definitely affected that.

I think it was a combination of me not being very forceful, but also his mule-like stubbornness, and preference for only doing things his way.

We very rarely went head-to-head, as we were both quite laid back characters. Possibly due to his upbringing, he was not very good at showing emotion, which always infuriated Mum. Poor Dad, I got the impression he found growing up difficult in his early years, and it affected him in the latter.

Mum and Dad did have a good relationship generally, and it just 'worked', but they were polar opposites. As you know, my mum wore her heart very much on her sleeve, whereas my dad kept his buried deep under layers of clothing! (I think it was a combination of his real mother dying at a young age, and having a strict upbringing with his stepmum).

We left the hospital and walked back to the car park feeling quite deflated and dazed. I can remember having a million questions in my head, and thinking, so, what next?

I can only imagine how Mum's brain must have been; shocked, hugely concerned, confused, worried, and scrambled (even more so).

After all her previous comparatively trivial worries throughout her life, there was a real gigantic cause for concern now. Poor Mum.

It's at times like these you question life. You could think that life is not fair or just, but then again you know that other families have been through worse, and more. One thing I've learnt over the years, is that life isn't fair, and we shouldn't expect it to be. Hopefully, my kids have understood this from the various musings I used to write about in my weekly blogs as a personal trainer.

Life can appear unjust if you continually compare and contrast your life to others. There will always be people better off, wealthier, prettier, more successful, etc. but so what?

As they say, that's life!

It's far better to not worry about others, and look at improving yourself, your own life and your loved ones around you.

Yes of course Mum didn't deserve this, she wouldn't harm a fly, and had such a lovely gentle, caring nature, but you have to roll with the punches as they say (even if it was a complete sucker punch).

One huge epiphany for me, personally, was to look at life from the perspective of being grateful, and I have developed this even more so since my mum and dad's passing. You know the saying 'what does not kill you makes you stronger' - that definitely holds true for me.

I've always looked at life as a gift. I certainly don't take it for granted, and my love for life increases daily as a consequence of having gone through this experience. Seeing life in this way emphasises the notion that life is short, and we need to make the best of it while we can.

Going through the darker times, has made me appreciate *every* day - even the 'normal' hum-drum days!

When we arrived back at my parents' house, we did what any British person would do in these circumstances, and made a cup of tea. My mum's favourite, especially when combined with her favourite biscuits, like a chocolate Hobnob. There's just something so restorative about a cup of tea.

My mum used to call it 'nectar of the gods' (if only the gods could work a little bit harder on their miracles).

I felt so much for Mum, she was still in shock.

We tried to comfort her, and I know she appreciated

the support we offered just by being there, but what do you say to someone that's been diagnosed with this illness, knowing the way it develops? I guess it might be easier *not* to know in some ways, but in others you want to protect yourself and your loved ones, armed with the knowledge of how best to approach it.

I wanted to know, but then also I didn't, but as my dad used to say 'forewarned is forearmed'.

I did some research into Alzheimer's and cognitive impairment, and one study by the Oxford project investigating memory and ageing caught my eye. They used quantities of vitamins and minerals, namely: folic acid, vitamin B6 and vitamin B12, to control the levels of homocysteine in the blood. Findings suggest there are high levels of homocysteine in people with Alzheimer's.

The study set up a placebo group which had 'dummy' tablets and the others who took real supplements.

What they found when they compared the two groups after two years, was that the group taking the real supplements suffered 30% less brain atrophy. That's huge. I had to get Mum to try this.

I was always perplexed at the cost and quality of supplements, and their huge variance. Are the cheaper ones as effective as expensive ones?

I asked a lady I knew, who ran a health food shop for

years, and she recommended the 'Solgar' brand. (You might have seen the gold labelling?)

She had once been to the factory, saw it being made and was extremely impressed with their methods, ethos, and quality.

Interestingly, after a while of this intervention, the GP did a blood spectrum test and all the markers for each supplement measured high. They'd asked us what she'd been doing. When we explained, they said to stop immediately, as all her levels were way above the norm. (I also assumed there was a knock-on effect to other measurements within the blood test).

At this time, despite the Alzheimer's affecting her overall wellbeing, in comparison to the latter stages it was mild, although it didn't feel like it at the time. Much of the 'real Mum' was still present, but with more inconsistencies showing up.

There would be a few sentences forgotten and then repeated, some actions repeated, and she would appear vacant at times, but despite this, Mum tried to carry on as normal, as you would under the circumstances.

One worrying trait though, was she was getting more concerned with the physical aspects of everyday life. She began to have even more difficulty with stairs, was frightened to use them without help, and even then, under duress. Initially, we supported her and coerced, but it was starting to become obvious, that not only was her mind not prepared to go upstairs, she couldn't physically manage it on her own either.

Obviously, I wanted to do everything I could to help Mum, so I suggested that Dad bring her along to my personal training studio, and we could work on some physical training aspects, and keep her brain active too. My thought was that a healthy body will make a healthy mind.

The benefits of exercise and movement are well known both for mind and body, and I wanted her to have some of these, as a support mechanism, alongside the medication and my help.

It actually worked out well for a while, as I had coerced Dad to join in, and whilst I set him off with various tasks, I spent time with Mum giving her exercises, and trying to work a little on right and left-brain movements, focusing on coordination and spatial awareness.

I used different coloured cones for example and got her to touch different colours on demand. Sometimes it was just a little walking, sometime some strength work, together with some stretching, even a little bit of boxing! Nothing too brutal though, just patterns of punching for example.

I was also getting concerned with Mum's posture and

her gait. She seemed to be losing some postural muscle tone and leaning forward more. She was struggling to lift her feet. She started to develop the start of what we called the 'Alzheimer's shuffle'. If you have seen someone doing it, you will know what it looks like.

I'd like to think that some of the work we did together helped, and maybe kept some of the effects at bay if only for a short time, but sadly we knew we were fighting an uphill battle, as the condition took further hold.

Regardless of this though, it was lovely to see them both regularly, catch up and have social time together. I could check up on them both and it was nice for them to get out of the house, and change focus. The benefits of social contact here too, cannot be underestimated, both for the brain and overall wellness.

I really felt for Dad. Whilst he was well known for using big words and complex vocabulary, he was also a quiet reserved man, who internalised his feelings and issues rather than talking them through. He was a great thinker. In fact, I swear you could hear his brain whirring sometimes!

He was well known for his wit and intellect and did have a very dry sense of humour.

From what I understand, each person with Alzheimer's

can be affected in quite different ways. There may be similarities, but maybe a different order or different magnitude of effects. Aside from the forgetfulness, repetition, and appearing vacant, Mum was starting to be affected more physically. She was having some difficulty walking, and was definitely losing confidence in moving around generally.

She had also just started to feel like she needed to go to the toilet all the time, and at some of our personal training sessions, a lot of time was being taken up with repeatedly visiting the toilet.

Dad spoke to the Doctor about this, and she was given some medication to diminish the sensation.

Unfortunately, this loss of sensation resulted in her having 'accidents'.

The issue here, was not only was she confused about what was happening, but was wondering why Dad was cleaning her up, as, in her own mind, nothing had actually happened.

Despite him dealing with this well, it must have been very tough. He was starting to take on more of a 'carer' role, and that must have been a very difficult transition. Dad said that sometimes Mum, after messing herself, would run off around the house, confused, obviously spreading mess elsewhere. What a nightmare for him.

We set about getting suitable nappies, and it was trial and error finding the right ones that were both comfortable and didn't leak. We sourced some online, and bulk bought as they were not cheap.

Mum did initially get some through the NHS, but they were few and far between, didn't last long and weren't the best for her individual needs.

Things were escalating, and with Christmas coming we wanted them to be with us, so we could keep a close eye on them.

CHAPTER FOUR
CHRISTMAS AND BEYOND

I won't forget this particular Christmas, but not necessarily for the right reasons. It was an incredible eye opener, because we could see exactly what Dad was dealing with, day-to-day, caring for Mum.

He did *everything* for her. He dressed and undressed her, fed her, washed her and changed her nappies. It was shocking how much she had regressed.

We knew we could not let him go back to their house alone with Mum and carry on like this. He didn't want intervention and was adamant he could cope, but we thought otherwise, despite how brilliant he had been.

Whilst at our house Dad had given the GP our telephone number so he could check on how things were. When the phone went and he answered, I did earwig and listen, but it was just to check everything Dad said was correct. In my eyes, I had his best interests at heart.

I couldn't believe my ears. Dad was telling him that yes, he is fine, and we are all coping well, and Mum was doing as well as could be expected! I heard the GP ask if he needed any more support and he said, "No, because Stuart and Lisa are helping"! I'm normally very even tempered but uncharacteristically, I blew a fuse, got very cross and said, "Bullshit Dad, bullshit!"

I think the realisation of what was happening, together with the raw emotions had got the better of me.

I said to Dad, that he did need help, and desperately!

We would obviously support him as much as we could, but he needed more help than we could offer. We just couldn't give them both as much support as they needed right now, and would need in the future (cue guilt complex).

I felt awful at being so hard-line, but he did need help and quick. His pride, however would not allow him to ask for external support.

On reflection, I can understand where he was coming from. He had promised Mum he would take care of her, and it was almost as if he hadn't fulfilled his promise. I think he also felt like he *should* be able to cope with it all. This made me so sad because he really had been amazing.

After our earlier conversation/heated argument and the realisation of what Dad was dealing with, we had reached another crisis point, where things had to be actioned, and urgently.

The next day we all decided we needed to get some fresh air (perhaps to clear the air), so we went to the lovely nearby seaside town of Clevedon. Mum, Dad, Lisa, me, the kids, and Lisa's parents Sue and Bo.

It's a beautiful Victorian town, with a lovely promenade but is also most famous for its pier, and swimming lake.

It was one of those bright, crisp blue-sky days where we all got wrapped up and decided to go for a little stroll and stretch our legs. We supported Mum and didn't go too far, but on our return she had great difficulty getting back into the car. It was as if she had no control at all.

It didn't help that it was in my dad's pride and joy, his Peugeot RCZ. It was low and had sporty seats (it was more than a midlife crisis car, more like a later life crisis car - is that a thing?!).

I'm pretty strong luckily, but it did take some considerable effort to get her: a) in the car and b) sitting upright correctly and in the right position.

Looking back, issues tended to come in blocks and sometimes we went from emergency to emergency. Firefighting comes to mind, as suddenly there would be a massive issue, then it might be calm for a little while.

When the issue was resolved, suddenly another critical issue would arise which needed to be resolved. And so on (that rollercoaster again).

One such occurrence was that Dad had to do more manual handling and he was struggling to cope, physically. I would get calls in between training my clients, where Dad would say, "Your mum's on the floor and I can't lift her up."

So, I had to drop everything, let clients know what was going on, and race over to help. I felt awful knowing that Mum was on the floor for the duration of my drive over.

This was obviously stressful and worrying. At work I was about 40 minutes away, but home was an hour and 10 minutes.

It got to the stage where Mum was starting to lose overall strength in her legs, becoming unable to support herself. I'm sure her brain was also impacting the physical - being unable to send the right signals and get the muscles to fire in the right order and respond correctly. With these issues rearing their ugly heads and Mum getting weaker, she had stopped going to the gym, so I wasn't seeing them as frequently as I had before. I was surprised how quick these recent changes had impacted on both Mum and Dad's lifestyle.

I told Dad he had to get help; that it couldn't carry on

like this, and with huge relief, he saw sense and agreed - phew!

The GP had organised a community support nurse to come and help but it was clear even greater help was a needed. We researched support and arranged for a company to come and help them, at least in getting Mum up, and putting her back to bed. That at least lessened Dad's manual handling duties and meant it was a little easier for him to deal with the day. It was actually good company for him too, as he had someone to just talk day to day chit-chat with.

He had some savings and his pension, and was using that to supplement support - thank goodness he was able to afford it, as I don't know what would have happened otherwise.

The next firefighting episode made us also realise that Mum needed a wheelchair, and quick. She was losing confidence in her walking abilities and along with it, her ability to control her muscles.

Luckily, there was a mobility shop in Burnham-on-Sea where I live, so we were able to buy a wheelchair that was in stock, that very day. One issue solved. I feel sure she might have been able to get a wheelchair through the NHS, but we needed it, yesterday.

If you get a chance to look in these types of shops, they have a myriad of tools and gadgets that can really help those experiencing mobility or dexterity issues and they were extremely helpful. Little did we know at that point we would be back shopping for Dad in a few years.

We also bought Mum a 90-degree angle spoon to make it easier for her to feed herself, and some beaker cups with lids that minimised spillages.

Looking back, you just deal with what's thrown at you, as it comes, but emotionally it's a rollercoaster ride, and a big one at that.

Dad soon realised too, that he had to get rid of his beloved sports car, and get a wheelchair accessible car that would be suitable for transporting Mum. That must have been tough. You certainly couldn't get much more of a contrast between the two cars, but to his credit, he took it all in his stride.

To make things easier I went over with him to the local 'We buy any car' and signed the car over. I did feel a tinge of sadness for him when he handed over the keys, but 'needs must'.

There was a specialist wheelchair car company not that far away, in Swindon, that would come to you with a car, making the logistics way easier. Dad booked them to come over and chose a Peugeot Teepee, where Mum could be safely transported in the back without leaving her wheelchair. This afforded them some freedom to go out and to come over to us.

Despite the additional help at home, and now the new vehicle to transport Mum in her wheelchair, I think Dad was starting to experience a shift in his thinking. One thing we had discussed, intermittently weaved within other conversations, was the prospect of them both moving to be closer to us, so we could support more.

They were only just over an hour away, but he must have been thinking of where we were, and that the level of support needed would only increase.

I know he was very appreciative of our help, but I do think he was thinking of support not just for Mum, but for him too, so it definitely made sense.

I am so pleased to say that he agreed to our idea and actioned it. Things were definitely moving in the right direction - literally!

Once their house was on the market, it didn't take long to sell, and I'm not surprised, as it was a beautiful, sought-after 17th century period cottage, with a more modern extension, good pavement appeal.

Mum had always kept the house looking nice, previous to her condition, and my dad was a modern man before his time, so he had helped around the house and garden. Interestingly enough now though, I had realised that it was Mum who had coordinated the garden, alongside my grandad.

Grandad Tom was an extremely knowledgeable gardener who knew all the Latin names and he had encouraged Mum to take an interest. Whilst Dad had helped, he didn't show as much interest, and his participation was generally with a gentle nudge from her.

We had quite a big task, to say the least to start clearing and emptying their house ready for the impending move however, mainly because my dad was from the era of not getting rid of <u>anything</u>.

1.5' 4x4 wood? Check.

2' copper pipe? Check

Broken chair that hadn't been mended for 20 years? Check.

All kept.

We needed to be more brutal in getting rid (I say we, but it was Dad).

We ordered a skip with the plan to fill it, but it was a complete battle to try and get anything in it! Every piece was a discussion and a deliberation, which took way longer than it should have. I used all my powers of persuasion and coercion, to 'help' him get rid of stuff. He was definitely attached.

By some miracle, more went in than I had initially anticipated.

Inside the house, I remember emptying the kitchen cupboards, and I did find that particularly hard for some reason. I think mainly because it reminded me of all the baking and cooking Mum had laboured on over the years, and there would of course, be no more of that.

It made me think of the cooking sessions that she had done with Ella and Josie, the scones and cheese straws, the cupcakes, and just general making a mess - the girls loved it as much as Mum did.

She absolutely loved making and baking and put a lot of effort into dinner parties and family gatherings; it was her way of showing she cared for and loved the recipients. We were also very appreciative, because she was an excellent cook.

All that had stopped with Mum's inability to function as she once did. That must have been both frustrating, confusing and frightening, and I hoped that the realisation transitioning to forgetting wasn't too long.

It's difficult to estimate how long it the transition from 'real Mum' to 'Alzheimer's Mum' actually took, as it was both slow and quick, for physical and mental faculties, respectively.

I think back to when we all went to a swimming gala to cheer on my lot, who were all avid swimmers. They swam for the local swimming club and were very proficient, learning all the strokes with ease.

I used to joke that I did depths rather than lengths when I went swimming, as I was definitely the weakest swimmer in the family!

I was a lifeguard many years ago, something my kids still can't quite believe, but I think it was my swimming technique in comparison to theirs that marked a clear distinction, as I never had formal lessons. Think demented washing machine, compared to well-oiled machine and you might get the picture!

I very rarely remember going swimming as a child, as Mum had apparently nearly drowned in the sea when she was a child, and from that point on was petrified of the water. Anyway, I'm digressing!

At the gala, my Mum sat next to a lovely lady, and I think she had sussed what was going on with her mentally, as Mum had asked the same questions over and over, and bless her, the lady answered each time, as it if it was the first.

As you might have gathered by now, my mum was a

very social person and loved chatting to anybody, so I think it really did do her good to be able to speak with others. What I wanted to highlight here however, was that whilst sometimes it was quite hard work going over and over what had been just said, and with Mum repeating herself, this was obviously way better than the silence and her inability to speak at all, which latterly, and sadly, was for quite a long period of time before her passing.

One thing I realised, as the Alzheimer's took more and more of a hold on her, is that you have to take each day as it comes. It's impossibly difficult if you focus on the future and what lies ahead, because it's a pretty depressing state of affairs. Small pleasures were welcome, so a chatty, engaged Mum was hugely better than a quiet or perplexed one, although as 'Alzheimer's Mum' took more of a hold, her personality was sadly starting to change.

We continued to empty and clear Spider Cottage, ready for the new occupants. I remember clearing out my nan and grandad's house after their passing and I hated it, as it made me feel empty within myself too.

Without them in it, the house was soulless, and going through and sorting all their worldly possessions was necessary and tough. This feeling was strangely similar - perhaps I was already grieving for the real Mum I was losing?

I do feel now, that you grieve for the person even before they've passed. The person you knew and loved, whilst there physically, is slowly slipping away. Mum changed immeasurably over the course of her journey.

You have memories, which together with photos offer great solace as reminders of times that once were. It's weird, but I see a picture of Mum laughing out loud and I can hear her, by just looking at the photo.

I think you emotionally attach to objects too, so I can see why Dad might have found it hard to get rid of `stuff.' When he saw these objects, it brought him some level of comfort and reminded him of the memories held within, providing solace as he reminisced on better times.

While the house was on the market, Dad had been looking at properties near to us, in and around Burnham-on-Sea. He had found a bungalow he liked and he put an offer in, which was accepted. It was a five-minute drive down the road from us - much quicker!

Little pleasures.

As we continued to work towards a moving date, Dad had been sent a message from the owner of the house they were moving to. In simple terms, despite a price being agreed previously, they were informing him that they had in fact been offered another higher offer, which she had decided to accept. Would Dad like to up his offer again?!

Whaaatt?!!

I absolutely hate this lowball stuff. Legal, but unscrupulous. My Dad, despite feeling the pressure now, did what I would have done too, stuck two fingers up and said on your bike! (Metaphorically speaking).

Thankfully it didn't take long for him to find another property, and the bonus: it was even closer to us!

CHAPTER FIVE
THE NEW HOUSE

In the great scheme of things, it didn't take long for moving day to arrive, so it was all hands on deck to get their house more liveable.

My Uncle Ian very kindly assisted by putting up boards in the loft, to hold the mountain of stuff that didn't make it into the skip.

It was obvious at this point that there was still way too much, even after the cull. What the hell were we going to do with it all?!

Spider Cottage had been way bigger, and they had to downsize. It's just that Dad didn't want to downsize his possessions.

Luckily the new house had three bedrooms, albeit smaller ones, and we were also able to pile boxes in other areas, together with some going into a local storage unit.

Mum and Dad were in, and were much closer to us.

We felt more reassured that we could offer more support when needed, and although he didn't say it directly, I know Dad felt better about things too.

One of the main factors to consider when moving, was to ensure there was a safe, efficient and effective transfer of Mum's care. We had already registered them both with the local GP, and had found a care company to assist in their home. Mum was also under the watchful eye of a community nurse, and there was a social worker involved in her case.

Dad dealt with all the financials, but I believe there was some support financially towards her care, hence the local authority input.

It felt so much better with my mum and dad being closer.

We were seasoned 'firefighters' by now, and were certainly used to dealing with the odd crisis, but it was more comforting for us all to know that we could react quicker, when the time came.

Mum had transitioned well, considering the major upheaval. She had declined a little more overall but that was to be expected. She was now in a wheelchair permanently and didn't walk. She needed constant care, to be dressed, fed, and have her nappies changed.

She had started to put on weight. The reasons were

two-fold. Firstly, she wasn't moving around as she used to - she was either just sitting or lying down; and secondly, she would forget whether she'd eaten or not, and appeared to be a lot hungrier throughout the day. She demanded Dad get her something to eat - generally biscuits - together with her beloved cup of tea!

I also noticed that the muscles we had worked hard to preserve earlier in the journey were also starting to atrophy. This is the classic 'if you don't use it, you lose it' syndrome, where because muscles are not being used, they waste. As muscles use up calories actively, for every pound of muscle lost, it meant her metabolism was slowing also. Each compounded the other, so she was losing muscle, and gaining fat.

Throughout her life she had always been concerned with her overall bodyweight and had spent all her life dieting - you name it, she had done it - FPlan, Cabbage Soup, Weight Watchers, Slimming World, etc. and she used to buy all those classic seventies diet items, such as reduced calorie Slimcea bread and Tab Cola, Coca Cola's first diet drink.

Now though, she was oblivious to her weight gain, and had no concerns about food choices or amounts. In some ways it was liberating to see her enjoy her food without restricting herself or worrying, but not under these circumstances.

Dad walked a tightrope between appeasing her and not over feeding, which was not easy by any means. She was now starting to get a little tetchy at times, which was a concern. From what I understand, mood changes are to be expected, but how it manifests varies person to person. Sometimes it can be an extension of their original personality, and other times a total departure. Mum was the latter, although it must have been hugely frustrating and confusing, not being able to communicate as she wanted.

With both Mum and Dad going through so much, I wanted to give them both a nice surprise, and so it was with some of trepidation that I decided to buy them a kitten. I say trepidation as I wasn't too sure how they would react and whether it meant too much extra work.

They had cats before and absolutely loved them, and I reasoned that it might be a nice distraction for them both and offer some comfort. After searching the 'classifieds', I found one not too far away in south Wales. I apparently was the first to ring and so would have my pick of the litter. They were British shorthair and rag doll crosses so quite unusual, and I couldn't wait to see them.

When I arrived, I was ushered into a room with six beautiful kittens. Instantly I saw one with amazing markings, so I chose him. I couldn't wait to show Mum and Dad.

Luckily they took the surprise very well and were over the moon. We said Mum should name him, and after a lot of coaxing she actually said a name – Henry!

Henry settled in well, and loved sitting around Mum's shoulders when she sat in her chair, which she really enjoyed. Perfect!

Mum had been quite prim and proper really. She was very down to earth, extremely friendly, and always had a nice appearance. She enjoyed her clothes and dressing well, and her hair was just so, although she always moaned that she couldn't get it the way she wanted. She always had a lot of hair that was very curly, and in her eyes unmanageable, much to her annoyance.

In the 60s she had a beehive, and in later years her hair was always styled quite big. I think she would have preferred straight hair, but from what I believe for a lot of people where hair is concerned, you tend to want the opposite of what you were born with!

Dad was very good at continuing her grooming. He ensured her nails were manicured and occasionally painted. He organised a lady to come in to do this, who I actually knew from one of the health clubs I worked in, small world. He also organised a hairdresser to come round, which Mum enjoyed, but by which time she was also understandably occasionally confused.

The new care team were coming in regularly to see Mum, initially twice a day, going up to three times a day. It was a blessing for Dad to get help, but it also added some extra comfort and company. It helped to give his day some structure; such a small thing, but it helped to provide a framework which he could work around, something he had been used to during his service in the RAF.

I was in awe of the care team. They made such a huge difference to our lives, on many levels. In my eyes they are the unsung heroes.

They dealt with Mum with great dignity and care and spoke kindly to her, asking how she was as well as general chit-chat. In the earlier days they would be two-way dialogues, but that sadly was starting to diminish.

They knew though to still to speak to Mum, explaining what was happening to her and what they were doing, despite not knowing how much was being processed.

They were always cheerful, despite workloads, and gave excellent service, all for minimum wage through their company. They deserved a lot more, but we weren't allowed to give them anything extra, under company policy. They were our eyes and ears and fed-back to me regularly. They kept a log of everything they did, and would write comments about how Mum was, what she'd eaten and drunk, and her general demeanour. It helped us immensely and was incredibly comforting to know that someone else was keeping an eye out as well. That included Dad too actually, as if they had any concerns with him, they would let me know.

Whilst the carers were explaining what they were doing to her, I think Mum was still finding it bewildering and confusing. Poor Mum.

You can certainly understand it because they were bed washing her and cleaning her intimately.

We did find, because of this, that she was starting to voice a reaction, shouting and swearing.

Well, I don't think I'd ever heard her swear, ever, she would have been mortified. "You f*cking bitch, you fat cow, what do you think you are doing?!"

At some level, I was mortified to hear such language, but on another stronger level, I felt so sad that Mum was evoking almost an 'animal' knee jerk reaction to, in her eyes, someone being invasive.

She had also started to swear at Dad too, which was very distressing for him. Despite knowing there was no malice, it was incredibly difficult not to take it to heart. It tended to be when she didn't understand what was being done to her, so for instance Dad getting her strapped in to the car. "What are you f*ckin doing, leave me alone. I hate you!" So very, very, sad.

I also knew my mum didn't mean any of these words at all, and I know the staff knew this too, but it must have still been very hard to ignore these comments.

Here, sadly, we see 'Alzheimer's Mum' taking precedence and 'real Mum' diminishing. This could, and did change day-to-day, and some days were better than others, which was a mixture of happiness and heart wrenching at the same time.

On some days, I would see flashes of the old real Mum and you could get her to engage and be more 'present', but on other days she was vacant and distant. A teasing glimpse into what once was. Strange how it would happen, and there would be no rhyme or reason as to when.

Whilst I was extremely happy to see and feel the old Mum was still there, it was almost as if Alzheimer's was goading me. To see a glimpse of what was, and then have it snatched away. It felt tougher than her staying the same, but of course we took at least some solace from what felt like, genuine engagement. Cruel.

Whilst we were reluctantly accepting what Mum was going through, it did make me think what a truly wicked condition this was. Her decline appeared slow and painful to endure. Dad, the rest of the family, and me were mere observers to what she was going through. At that point I actually hoped, for her sake, that she was less present, so that she was able to cope better.

I tried not to dwell too much on the thought of the real Mum battling the confusion, trying to make sense of what was going on, but the thought was always present.

So, with Mum being less mobile and her recent weight gain, bedsores became an issue. To cut a long story short Dad organised, through the community nurse, a proper hospital bed and hoist for her bedroom. This helped the carers with manual handling, could be adjusted easily, and they could also use an air mattress to minimise bed sores.

The other thing we found was that with Mum's increased weight, she was having difficulty fitting into her existing wheelchair. Dad, again, sorted this and bought it independently, to speed the process up. Not cheap at £2,000 but essential. It was a million times more comfortable and infinitely more adjustable. We were lucky that Dad had the funds to do this, and he obviously felt it was money well spent.

We were definitely getting better at this firefighting business.

Lisa and I were always checking in with Dad and kept a close eye on him. We knew it was extremely tough to watch the person you love and cherish change before your very eyes. Lisa would pop in to see him, and sometimes take him out for lunch, or stay with Mum while he went out, and I know he appreciated the company, the chat and the help.

I remember him saying that he missed the little off hand comments, like, "Look at this, what do you think?" Or, "I see so and so is going to wherever it might be." Of course, now there was very little back and forth with Mum.

I had earmarked Monday mornings into early afternoon every week to help Dad, so I'd stay and let him go out shopping or do whatever he wanted. Both Lisa and I also sat with Mum at various times, so that he could get out of the house and enjoy some freedom.

We were very concerned at the enormity of Dad having to deal with this on so many levels, but especially emotionally. We found it very draining, so we were trying to imagine how he must have felt. We were only dealing with this in the wings, as opposed to living within it 24/7 as he was.

We realised he needed more independent time too, for his own sanity, and it was arranged that for one day a week Mum would go into a local care home to have a shower, be fed, and have different stimulation. He paid for this day out of his own money, but it was so desperately needed.

He started to go to aircraft museums and do some of the things he used to enjoy, which was fantastic, as it lifted his spirits and gave him something to plan and look forward to.

I tried to encourage him to meet others, and get involved socially, with at least something. I found a local walking group, which he did on a Monday when I could stay with Mum. I was elated when he agreed to do it because I knew how much good it would do him, both physically and mentally.

The way to work around Dad with these things was to talk about it, show all the details and benefits and then leave it. Later I would bring it up in conversation again, until he decided to bite the bullet. There was no enforcement, just very gentle persuasion.

The other benefit of Mum having one day a week in the care home was that they knew her, and it appeared that some of the staff were becoming very fond of her, despite her limited communication. So, she had a new environment, new stimulation, new friends, different food, and the level of care she needed.

Dad was allowed to apply for some local authority funding to help get him longer respite care for her. He could then have one week away, and we were so pleased for him that he wanted to take it. Of course he deserved, and needed it, but I thought it might be an uphill battle to persuade him to do so. Thankfully, not.

The weeks of respite breaks gave him something even more exciting to plan and look forward to, and it was lovely to see him planning his outings with military precision. His first few trips were aircraft based, of course!

Dad, being an ex-RAF man, had a real passion for world war aircraft, and loved nothing more than going to an old airfield, war museum, or anything remotely linked to aircraft in any way.

As expected, Mum was starting to have real issues and more round-the-clock care was being needed. She was getting noisier and more vocal at night, and it was affecting Dad's sleep. He bought a night monitor to listen out for her, but it was understandably affecting his overall wellness.

At the same time, she was having more bed sore issues, despite the air bed, and needed turning more often than she currently was. This was a major issue. They looked so painful and some of them made huge blisters. She was in pain, but then didn't fully understand why.

She now couldn't verbalise what the issue was effectively, and got so frustrated and cross. I was always so shocked at how quickly these blisters could materialise, and it was a real concern.

Obviously as well as the carers, the local authority had a concern in Mum's care, and we didn't understand the ramifications at the time, but when she was reviewed, they were concerned with her overall health and care package. They realised at that point, that Mum's needs meant a greater level of care was required than she was currently getting.

We didn't know this at the time, but this meant Mum being taken into care, full time, outside of their home.

Bearing in mind what Dad had promised Mum, i.e. that he would care for her in their own home, and that she wouldn't go into care, you can begin to understand the magnitude of this.

In fact, this did us all a favour because Mum desperately needed more full-time care, and because of her declining health this was now taken out of Dad's hands.

He had no choice. It wasn't his decision to make. In some ways this made it slightly easier, but it was still desperately sad for him.

It wasn't a 'should she, shouldn't she', he was told point blank - Diana is going into a home, so she can have the care she needs at this present time. There wasn't a timeframe put on it, just that she needed to get fully better first, before a decision was made for her next stage.

Little did we know, that was the last time she would be in her own home.

Luckily, she went into the same home where she had received respite care - Holywell Nursing Home. The staff there were brilliant, and they had thorough knowledge of Alzheimer's and dementia, and knew how to deal with Mum.

As you can imagine, the thought of Dad being on his own in the house now was also a great concern. I was well aware that his health had declined as a consequence of being Mum's carer, despite the extra help. I think the physical and the mental anguish had exacted a price.

Dad had some concerning health issues. He had already been through three different cancers, and some pretty heavy chemotherapy.

After the first diagnosis and operation, where he was told he had 6 weeks to live, he felt they hadn't bothered to stitch him up perfectly, knowing the probable outcome. Who knows? Whatever the truth, he had a weakness, and now a hernia, so he had to be extremely careful not to exert and put pressure through that area.

He had about 16% kidney function which brought about lots of other issues. He was extremely tired all the time, and had to have twice weekly checks for blood, as he was on the blood thinning medication Warfarin. I took him to his appointments on a Monday and tried to rearrange my personal training clients for the others. Lisa also helped and sometimes Lisa's parents too, whilst we continued to juggle life in general.

I can't say he looked after himself that well, and it was a bit of a battle to get him to eat the right foods. He loved his food, but just ate whatever he fancied, which was not the most nutritious, to say the least.

His favourite foods were exactly the things he shouldn't have been eating, so he ate lots of crisps - sodium, and chocolate - sugar, and hardly any vegetables, lots of white bread, etc. so I was worried he wasn't getting good nutrients.

I get it, he was eating for pleasure but in the long term it wasn't helping him.

Whilst talking about food, one thing I haven't mentioned was the 'healthier' ready meals for ease (if that's not an oxymoron) that Dad had arranged while Mum was still at home.

After a bit of research Dad found the company, Wiltshire Farm Foods, and as ready meals go, they were tasty and pretty good nutritionally. It made food preparation easier for both of them, so it was worth it for that alone.

Mum was developing very specific food requirements due to limited chewing and swallowing responses. Wiltshire Farm Foods offered different graded levels of consistency, mashed or liquidised, to minimise a choking response and aid swallowing. It also saved a lot of time in food preparation and hassle for Dad.

They delivered them frozen to the house, and I found out afterwards, even put them in the freezer for him. The good thing about this was, at least he had some nutritious food in him. (Although it was clear he didn't always eat the healthier aspects of the meal, sometimes vegetables being left).

Even liquids that could be swallowed too quickly had to be thickened, to ensure Mum didn't choke. All her drinks, hot or cold, had an added thickening agent.

Around this time unfortunately, there was also something else unsavoury going on in the background, which we didn't find out about until I noticed an issue when I was looking through Dad's cheque stubs, which he left out when sorting his financials.

There was a name that kept coming up for multiples of hundreds of pounds, and then quite a few blanks with large amounts added at the bottom, so I questioned Dad what these sums were for. This chap was doing odd bits of gardening, for a few hours at a time and was charging £200/£300/£350 etc.

His name was on multiple stubs, and it was starting to all add up to quite a sum. Then I had noticed some much larger sums over £1,000 and more, and asked Dad what that was for. He said some chaps had come and said there were roof tiles that needed replacing and his rear wall needed repointing, etc.

Well, it was blooming obvious to me what was happening, that the word was getting round that there was a soft touch in the neighbourhood rife for ripping off. There had been no tiles which needed replacing or walls needing repointing, and he had been charged nearly £3,000 for the privilege. The gardening work, in the loosest sense was being charged at £100's of pounds per hour.

This made me so cross! How do these people live with themselves?!

Simply no morals or remorse it seems.

We did get the police out, and it was an actual name that they recognised, but it was an alias. The chap had asked Dad to leave the actual name on the cheque blank.

I put a 'no cold callers' sign up on the front door and I put a dummy video recorder up. It seemed to lessen the visitors. Despite this, and the neighbours looking out, we still had a caller requesting that Dad pay him, for the imaginary work he supposedly did last week. Thankfully, Dad said he had no money to give him, and that it had all gone, and amazingly it pretty much stopped there.

We read about a similar case in our local paper afterwards, where a pensioner got hit with a hammer, but luckily survived, and it was the same name Dad had on his cheque stubs!

It doesn't even bear thinking about.

CHAPTER SIX
HOLYWELL

Holywell Nursing Home, where Mum was now residing, was a lovely old Victorian property, nestled in the foothills of Brent Knoll. A beautiful setting and only two miles away from both Dad and I.

She had been given her own room, so it was important that it felt homely and welcoming to her. We still didn't know how much she would recognise or remember, but we obviously wanted to make the effort regardless.

I made up a photo frame with pictures of Mum, not all for her benefit though, as I wanted the staff there to get an inkling as to the type of person she was before Alzheimer's took hold. I knew the staff were incredibly considerate and caring already, but I thought it might help on some level. We made sure that the TV and radio worked. She didn't have the attention span to watch TV, but even some background noise was better than silence.

I always made sure she had plants and fresh flowers in her room. As Mum had been a florist I thought the familiar sights and smells would comfort her. Although I did read that smell can be one of the first senses to diminish it was still worth a try. In the early days she did react when I placed flowers near her nose, later she opened up her mouth, thinking it was food.

Remembering Mum's affection for all things festive, I put Christmas lights in there as well, together with baubles and tinsel to add to the effect.

Who cares if it wasn't Christmas?

As she was lying down a lot, I bought a projection light which lit up the ceiling and moved around with different colours. Anything to provide some stimulation.

We even bought her a room diffuser and used various essential oils.

By now, she was less reactive or communicative. We paid close attention to her non-verbal communication and body language to gauge how she was.

One huge factor, which was always at the back of our minds, was at what point she might not recognise us. It was something that Dad had spoken to me about, which meant he was concerned, as he normally kept his cards close to his chest.

Dad had been so strong for Mum, and I was very concerned for how it must have felt, being separated from her. I remember him implying he didn't like going to Holywell. Obviously, he loved to see and be with Mum, but I understood his reticence, as I too often experienced a 'feeling in my tummy' beforehand, and felt drained and a little low after.

I feel awful admitting that now, but on reflection it's a normal human response. I loved her dearly and I think it was all part of the grieving process.

It was hard not to, but when I looked at the photos I'd chosen for her wall, I'd think of much better, more carefree times. The contrast was stark.

Dad visited Mum regularly initially, but I know that he found each visit tough.

Whenever he visited her, it was a difficult reminder of everything he'd lost. Yes, she was *there*, and there was sometimes a reaction, depending on how she was feeling, but it was very hard just being an observer, watching her ever so slowly decline.

Painful.

He didn't know what to say to her sometimes, so he would read a book to her, which was endearing.

I think back to those days when Mum would just chat, repeat and express herself, and it was now in huge contrast, to the much quieter, more withdrawn Mum. I missed those chattier times.

More often now, I looked for eye contact or even better a smile. It was so lovely to get a smile, it brightened my whole day. Little pleasures.

We put some soft toys in Mum's bedroom too. Two cats, one reasonably lifelike, and a Bagpuss! (Remember the children's programme?)

To my surprise Mum reacted to one and started talking to it, "Hello, how are you?!" she said. She really thought it was real. You could have knocked me over with a feather! You never know what goes on in the brain, and this just shows what some stimulation can do.

Dad set up a payment plan for her care, and he did get some local authority contribution, but it was still a fair bit of money going out. Luckily, he had planned for his future and set up pensions, ISAs, etc.

I always found the money side of things so impersonal because they had to talk very frankly about Mum's life expectancy, in relation to organising funding to suit her needs and timeframe. Obviously, it was a necessary conversation, but I felt like saying, "Hey! There's a human behind this! This is my mum you are talking about!"

The home was perfect for her because she needed

round the clock attention, and I was able to see what she ate, drank, and how she was at any time by looking through the logbook, which the staff filled in, just like the carers had back at home.

I got quite friendly with some of the staff there, and I have to say they were all lovely. Such genuinely caring, lovely people.

I'd like to think I could do their job, but a lot of the residents are coming to the end of their lives, and I know they create such a bond with these people, it must be very tough not to take home what happens during the work day.

It was a great comfort to all of us, including close relatives, to know that Mum was in good hands within Holywell care home. I can't praise the staff enough, they were all so committed, with genuine empathy.

They were cheerful, which I can only imagine must be an effort considering the resident's stage of life, and the ailments they had, but it was infectious and gave the home have a lovely feel and atmosphere. I did understand it though - they knew they were improving all their residents' lives - they were making a difference.

It reminded me of a hotel I once worked at where in the staff room, just before going into the main hotel, was a sign saying, "You're on stage now - smile!"

Here though, this wasn't forced or artificial. It was genuine and from the heart.

Mum's muscle wastage was getting more pronounced now and she was becoming skeletal. She was more skin and bone than anything else and her muscle had all but gone. It was a shock to see what was left of her. She always wanted to be skinny, paradoxically, but I feel quite confident not in any way like this.

We had several scares where a chest infection meant Mum struggled to breathe, with a pronounced chesty cough and high temperature. She was very poorly.

Every time the home called, and I saw their number on my mobile, I felt physically sick. Often though, it was the lovely lady from accounts asking for a top up on Mum's petty cash account. She always made a point of saying before anything else, that there were no issues, and not to worry, as she knew the potential effect a call from that number would have.

I was starting to lose count of the number of times, where I thought, 'Ok, you need to prepare yourself Stuart', and then she miraculously recovered. I'd even been told by the staff to expect the worst at times.

Such a huge rollercoaster, a really awful, adrenaline inducing, unbelievably shitty one.

What could I do? What *more* could I do? These were the questions I would always ask myself. I wanted to do the best for Mum, but was it ever enough?

I've realised now, that, yes, it was enough. I did the very best I could without compromising my responsibilities as a father, husband, son and personal trainer.

I always went in regardless on a Monday morning as a fixed appointment and took Dad with me. I generally also went in during the week or weekend depending on other commitments, but that was either just me or together with Lisa. (It somehow felt easier with Lisa).

Dad and I loved and adored Mum, but it's very tough watching someone you love so much just ever so slowly decline. I can see why they call Alzheimer's the long goodbye. It was a very painful, drawn-out goodbye.

We were now at the stage where we were unsure most of the time whether Mum recognised us. This is what we had been dreading.

There was an occasional smile, which very much brightened our whole day, but they were becoming more distant, as was she. The 'real Mum' was a faint outline and the 'Alzheimer's Mum' very much front and centre.

I always found it such a contradiction that the home

had a duty of care to ensure her health and wellbeing, whilst at the same time prolonging the inevitable. We all agreed that if Mum was a cat or dog she would have been put to sleep some while back.

It seems horrible to even write that because I'm talking about my beautiful mum; the woman that wiped away my tears, comforted me, supported me at the drop of a hat, and gave me that rare and wonderful thing - unconditional love; but it was hugely painful to just sit and watch her fading away.

In summary, Mum did not speak, was extremely vacant, was a bag of bones (as my nan used to say), was on thickened fluids, liquidised/mashed food, frequently on antibiotics for a urine or chest infection, bed ridden, and doubly incontinent.

How was this fair?

Well, this combination must have been very concerning for the home too, as she was given end of life funding for her care, which pretty much said she was on her last legs.

The NHS lady who came and assessed Mum was lovely, but I found the whole impersonal nature of ticking off boxes and comparing all her issues from before to now, quite distressing. She discussed how many weeks of funding they might give and were basically trying to estimate when she might finally pass. To me, the human element was removed, and it was purely put down to the bottom line. Yes, I understand why, but it didn't make it any easier.

Well, in true Mum-style, over the next few weeks, we had several more heart pounding phone calls, where it was suggested we might want to come in, and then, just as we thought that was it, she would made a miraculous recovery. (We were back riding the shittiest of shit rollercoasters again - thinking about it, it would be quite apt, if it was Nemesis).

Family members likened her to an ox, and said she was a 'real fighter' but this certainly was no good thing, and I don't think she was conscious of her 'fight', much as we would all have liked to believe the real Mum was alive and kicking. It's really difficult to know what she was thinking, so I just prayed that she was in a happy place somewhere, or oblivious to the real-world struggle and pain.

We had more meetings with the NHS funding lady, and we went through more painful questioning and box ticking, after which they agreed to extend end-of-life funding, for just a little bit longer. In fact, it got to the stage where Mum had gone beyond end-of-life funding, if that's even a thing, or at least she had gone beyond the stage they were originally prepared to fund to. In their eyes she had stabilised.

In contrast to mum, who was getting the utmost in care, we were now getting more concerned with keeping an eye on Dad, especially as he wasn't in full health. There was no doubt about it he was getting increasingly fragile.

My dad was quite a formal person, possibly stemming from his RAF background, but one thing we had noticed was that he was not caring for himself as he once did.

Looking back at family get togethers, he tended to wear a suit and tie, and his 'informal' dress was a cravat!

So, it was a bit disconcerting when we found he'd worn the same clothes a number of days running with accumulated food stains, or he hadn't shaved, or even got up.

In part we felt that he was giving up. This was worrying.

We were getting more concerned for his mental outlook and now added to this his physical abilities. I think he was in a state of apathy and didn't feel like doing anything. His lack of movement was causing the same problems that had plagued Mum, atrophy of muscles and therefore diminished strength.

He had a few minor falls, which he played down as unusual occurrences or anomalies, but for Lisa and I, they were a big red flag.

After a lot of coaxing and badgering I persuaded Dad

to go to the mobility shop with me, and just 'look' at the four wheel walkers.

I said, "You don't have to buy one, just try it and see how you get on." (Hoping that once he was there he might like it, or I might be able to use my powers of persuasion on him!)

Well, my luck was in, because he tried it and actually liked it! Hoorah!

I think the clincher was a that it had a seat, where he could rest when tired and had brakes to keep control of it.

The shop assistant also recommended a walking stick with prongs on the end (think like the old guy in the film 'UP', but without the tennis balls on the ends!).

We now had two things that would minimise him falling, all we had to do now was to make sure he used them!

Yes, you can imagine that took a bit of work too, and a few more minor falls.

Here's where I had to apply a bit of pressure because I said to him if he continued to fall, and not use his aids, then he might not be able to live independently. The decision would be taken out of his, and our hands and the local authority would step in.

It was a weird one, this role reversal, but I had to do it, for his own benefit.

As an added safety net to the carers, he got an Aster pendant to go around his neck, so that if he did fall, he could press the button and it would call the emergency office. He could then speak into the phone unit from wherever he was in the house and they would take the appropriate action. (You won't be surprised to know it was a battle to get him to actually wear it, despite the benefits!).

Well, he did use his walking aids, albeit intermittently, but just occasionally he'd 'forget' and on one of these occasions, a carer found him in the hallway one morning, pretty much naked, unable to get up. According to Dad, he hadn't been there long, but I wasn't too sure.

The carer, Gordon, rang me and relayed what had happened and I wondered why he hadn't pressed his button. I quickly found out it was because whilst he did have it on, he'd asked the carer to ring me directly, and ask not to call the ambulance, because I think he was scared of what might happen.

I had to make an executive decision and I chose to ring the ambulance because I didn't know if he was hurt. I came rushing back from work and went straight to the hospital.

Luckily, he was ok with no broken bones, but I didn't want to risk it further.

When he came home, we were all on high alert. The carers came in three times a day, and we kept an even closer watch.

I think this time his pride was hurt more than anything.

CHAPTER SEVEN
SPITFIRE TRAVELS

This book would not be complete without mentioning Dad's momentous day. It was a special day, and one that neither of us would forget.

It was something he had talked about as a bit of a 'pipe dream' really, but had never got around to organising, so over time, I applied some gentle pressure, and eventually he booked his dream trip!

As you've already gathered, Dad was a self-confessed world war aircraft nut. His service in the RAF had solidified a real passion for this era of aircraft.

He used to go to events like the Farnborough Air Show, I even went with him once, but his real passion was for aircraft from an earlier era.

He loved aircraft like Vulcans, Mosquitos, Hurricanes, Lancasters, and of course the Spitfire, you get the picture.

Dad subscribed to Fly Past magazine, to his old

squadron newsletter, and always had books on the go on anything related to this - technical, fiction and non-fiction. He had inherited some money in a will from a family friend, and he had discussed doing something with it, which we all heartily encouraged.

His dream was to fly one of these aircraft, but the costs involved, including getting the right insurances, meant there were very few options in the UK.

He had seen, in one of his magazines, a company based in Biggin Hill, Kent, a famous old wartime airfield, offering flights in a Spitfire. They were called flyaspitfire.com.

The place was unique. They had the world's largest collection of Spitfires. They offered Spitfire trips down to, and around the white cliffs of Dover - you don't get much more iconic than that!

We had to wait a while because of other previous bookings, and of course they didn't fly all year round, as it was all very weather dependant.

Trips were in high demand, which meant we had to wait a little while for our trip. After we booked, one trip was cancelled, which was very disappointing, but finally the day arrived.

The conditions and the weather looked pretty much perfect!

It was around about 2.5 hours' drive to get there, mostly motorway, and I was concerned to see how Dad would cope with the journey. He hadn't travelled that sort of distance for some time and he was quite frail at that point.

He was compos mentis, but had been having a few bowel issues, so we scheduled plenty of stops and I suggested he didn't eat too much prior to travelling.

The weather couldn't have been better on the way up - clear blue skies, a few puffy white clouds, lots of sun and great visibility and the roads were relatively clear.

I created a playlist of his favourite songs for our road trip - a mix of Jean Michel Jarre, Pink Floyd, Dire Straits, and some Michael Jackson thrown in for good measure.

We set off with Dire Straits blasting and I could tell Dad was buzzing. It was great to see him so animated happy. It was going to be the realisation of a dream and lifelong goal.

Once we arrived, we were greeted warmly by the organiser, and were told to go to the briefing room and watch a video about the process, what to be aware of, including how to eject and parachute out! (I'm glad to say that option was not needed!)

We were offered a cup of tea and a biscuit and Dad was measured up for his flight suit. We then went out to the viewing gallery and the decking platform looking over the airfield.

We spoke to some of the others that had also come for the trip of a lifetime.

I hadn't seen Dad so chatty and upbeat in a long time. It was like he had forgotten his cares and ailments and was just living in the moment. Of course, he was in his absolute element, and was very happy to educate others who were asking about the flight, and his background. He was extremely well read on lots of areas, but his favourite topic was aircraft of this type.

We were shown around the workshop and saw all the manufacturing areas. Incredible wings of aluminium with individually crafted and sectioned parts. Complete and incomplete engines and all the associated engineering.

What struck me was the size of the engines. To put things in perspective, I had driven up in a two litre Mini - these engines were 27 litre! What?! (Also, my Mini was 141 bhp compared to 1000 bhp!)

The work going on there was literally world class. Some people that happened to have a few million or so going spare, would deliver their dilapidated Spitfire to the workshop, then some while later, fly out in a pristine aircraft. (As you do).

Dad and I went back onto the viewing platform and he

was introduced to the pilot who would be flying. She was lovely, so warm and welcoming and answered all his questions.

The amazing fact about this particular Spitfire, was that there were two cockpits: one of only two in the world at that time, I believe. She said that it would be helpful for him to read and feed back some of the dual dials, and would he mind helping?

Would he?!!

We went down to the Spitfire together - I was in awe of being close to something so iconic. What an amazing machine.

I was a little concerned as to how easily Dad would get in and then out, but he had lots of help, and I'm sure as hell he wouldn't have missed it for the world.

You know what they say, "Where there's a will there's a way!"

I observed from a safe distance on the decking, looking over the airfield.

I imagined what it would have been like during World War II, as this was an important strategic airbase during the conflict. You could feel the history here.

He got set up and in. The pilot also got in. The ground staff did all the checks, and did what they had to do, to get the engine fired up.

Cough splutter, rev, cough splutter rev, a bit of smoke. A bigger cough and a splutter and there was a huge roar, as the engine came alive. And didn't it come alive!! Wow! I felt quite emotional for Dad. What a sound!

There was nothing comparable to the sound of that Rolls Royce Merlin engine being fired up.

I don't think I've ever heard an engine quite like that. Of course, I had heard the engine before, but on one of Dad's vinyl records!! (Yes he had aircraft engine records, of course!)

Chocks away! (I wish I had shouted that out then!)

The Spitfire was driven to the appropriate runway position, and with the throttle opened, it gradually picked up speed and started to lift up. Off it went up into the skies.

It made me think of all the brave pilots in the war taking off from this very field. I believe that Biggin Hill Airfield was of huge significance in the Battle of Britain. (Also a film favourite of Dad's).

He had paid a little extra to fly for 45 minutes and off they went to the iconic white cliffs on the southeast corner of England. Wow!

Unbeknown to me at that time, once Dad had been up a little while, and he had managed to take in the enormity of what was happening, the pilot had offered Dad control to fly it himself!! What?!!

This Spitfire had been adapted as a training plane, and so had dual controls. Wow! Dad was not only having a ride in it, he was flying it!!

A dream realised, right there.

I sat and pondered waiting for Dad to return, thinking about all that he had been through and how much he thoroughly deserved this experience.

I was absolutely made up for him, such a special moment and one I was so pleased to share with him.

I managed to film Dad taxiing back in, with that unmistakable engine sound. I still have it on my Instagram today. I felt quite emotional watching him come in, knowing how much it meant or him, especially with all the recent hardships.

I cherish that, and the photos. I am yet to find the recording of Dad actually flying, we think it's on a memory stick somewhere in his belongings.

Well, you know that saying, 'the cat that got the cream?' I reckon it was a 'lion with a huge vat of cream!'

I don't think he stopped grinning ear to ear, until he fell asleep on the way home!

The thing that struck me about the day was that it was like Dad was 40 years younger and had no concerns, no ailments, nothing wrong - amazing, and surprising in equal measure.

He chatted with likeminded people all about the trip, and about his life in the RAF, he was in his element!

I still have the spitfire travels playlist on my phone and occasionally I reminisce about the amazing day when my Dad morphed into an earlier version of himself and flew a Spitfire!

Wonderful memories. We did try and persuade him to do it again but alas it wasn't to be.

CHAPTER EIGHT
THE INCIDENT

After the bliss, happiness and excitement of the Spitfire trip, there was one occurrence, not that long after, that was probably a bit too much on the excitement stakes.

It frightened me and the rest of the family, to the absolute core. We didn't know then, but it was the start of many changes for Dad.

My dad had been invited to my Uncle Michael and Aunty Helen's home in the Cotswolds, (my mum's brother and wife) for an amazing experience, and he was so excited. A friend of theirs had a private aircraft (as you do!) and, knowing how much he enjoyed anything to do with aviation, invited him for a flying session. Now, obviously this didn't compare to the spitfire experience, but it was an amazing trip, nonetheless.

Lisa and I knew that he was doing this day and were both itching to find out how he got on.

We didn't hear anything until the next day strangely, when I had a phone call from Dad explaining, I quote, a 'funny' thing happened to me yesterday, and he paused. I waited with bated breath, yeeess?!

Dad: Well, you never guess what I did?

Me: No, what Dad?

Dad: Well, on my way back from the trip, I stopped at the services for a break.

He continued…

Dad: I came out of the services on the M5, and I went the wrong way to get back on the motorway.

Me: Hold on a minute, so you are telling me you went UP the southbound carriageway?!!!

Dad: Well, yes! I don't know how, and I got a bit confused, and I really don't know how it happened.

(Silence and disbelief, as I had to let my brain register what I'd just been told).

I think I said, "OH. MY. GOD." But my internal dialogue was going 'WHAT THE ACTUAL FUUCK!!!!'

Dad: Yes, funny, hey?!

Me: Mmm… funny?!!

O.M.G, O.M.G, O.M.G!!

Whilst I was still trying to comprehend what had happened, I had a million questions buzzing around in my brain.

Are you ok?

What happened?

How far did you get?

What did you do when you realised?

What time was this?

Did you get help?

I was trying to get a timeline and more information as to how it all transpired. Dad had also rung Lisa, as she was nearby, to try and go and collect his car. I was trying to relay what had happened to Lisa, and I think her face was probably just like mine - totally agog!!

Dad, worryingly, did seem a little confused as to how it all transpired. From his description it sounded like it was at Sedgemoor Services, which meant he was so close to home, as it was only one mile to his turn off. I wondered why he had stopped there when he would have been home in minutes?

Dad mentioned he had a lovely day, but that it took a bit longer than anticipated, but was still a bit unsure of the actual timeframes. We did feel he had got overtired from the long day and that had not helped in keeping his focus.

He remembered stopping at Membury Services, and we found a receipt to prove he had got fuel there. But why would he go back down the M4?

He had already asked me to help him collect his car,

explaining to me that the car was in the police pound in Yate.

Why would that be then, I asked?

I was trying to question him to get some answers, but he struggled to fill the gaps in his knowledge, which again was worrying.

Obviously at this point I was confused/perplexed/ concerned as to what to do next. With regards to what just happened, I didn't want him driving back, especially as I hadn't got the full picture yet.

Lisa took Dad and me over to the police pound, and they explained that he had to settle up four new tyres, which they had organised to get replaced.

Why, you may ask?

Because that's immediately what I was thinking? 'Why did he have to have all four tyres replaced?!'

Well, what a cracking question…

The answer…

It was because Dad had to be stopped on the motorway, by the Police, from driving any further, so they deployed a Stinger! Yes, you read that right – <u>a Stinger</u>! The extendable chain of spikes, that they throw in the path of stolen cars, to stop them.

Apparently, he had STILL tried to drive on after this, and several police cars proceeded to box him in, to literally force him to finally stop on the motorway. The whole M5 traffic had also been stopped to enable this manoeuvre to happen.

W.T.A.F.!!

We felt we needed to find the police officers who had dealt with the incident that night. After ringing around, Lisa managed to speak to the main officer, who had dealt with it.

Well, you couldn't make it up!

Dad had come out of Sedgemoor Services, and went *out* of the *entrance* and travelled against the flow of the night time traffic going *north* on the *southbound* carriageway, all the way up, to just past *Gordano* Services - travelling a total distance of 19.4 miles, in the dark, heading straight into the oncoming traffic!!

OMFG. OMFG.

How he or anyone else didn't get killed, I will just never know. It really doesn't bear thinking about!

After this incident, and Dad's confusion, we became increasingly concerned. There is absolutely no way this could ever happen again. Despite the police saying that if he drove again, they would charge him, he was adamant he wanted to drive. In his eyes, there was no way he was being forced to stop driving. No way. (Dollery obstinance).

Here lies a problem.

Dad, despite being a reserved quiet man, could be forceful when he had what my mum called, 'a bee in his bonnet.' (I think he had a nest.)

What could we do?

Firstly, I had to do something I found very difficult, and that was take his keys off him, including his spares. That was obviously for his own benefit because, despite the police warning, I really do believe he would have driven again. Secondly, we arranged for the policeman who dealt with the incident, to come round the house to explain where he stood.

There's no doubt he listened, but I was pretty certain, based on his answers and his demeanour, that he wasn't necessarily going to heed their warning.

Sadly for him though, that *was* the last time he drove. (Despite the fact I found letters, implying he was planning to do it again!).

The car was Dad's freedom and gave him the ability to go out and about, so it was a very bitter pill to swallow, to know he would lose that flexibility. I really felt for him.

I found the whole situation very challenging, but it had to be done.

Every time I now drive on that section of the M5, I think of Dad driving in the dark, facing the oncoming traffic. There's a blind summit section where the road is on two levels, Dad had remembered the police following him effectively parallel to him, they were on the M5 north and Dad on the M5 south. Wow.

He told me that the cars where flashing him, which was distracting him, and he seemed quite cross about it! It sounded like he was in the fast lane all the way. He couldn't explain why he didn't pull off onto the hard shoulder or why he didn't try and come off any of the other junctions.

I wonder how far north he would have gone, had he not been forced to stop.

From that point on we helped Dad whenever he needed to go anywhere - the doctor, get togethers, food shops, hospital appointments, library - you name it, we did it. It was hard work balancing that with kids and work, but it was worth it to ensure the same incident wasn't repeated.

CHAPTER NINE
DAD'S DIAGNOSIS

I felt I needed to dig a little deeper after the car incident.

Yes, he might have made a one-off mistake, but I felt if he was fully compos mentis, he would have not driven the distance that he did, and in that manner.

Just thinking about this now, gives me shivers, the 'what ifs', are inconceivable. For such an intelligent, logical man, something was not right.

I can't remember how I managed to persuade him now, which is strange, as I pretty much know it would have been a battle, (perhaps my brain blocked it out), but I arranged for Dad to be tested at the local Mulberry Memory Clinic. (Yes, I do realise how ironic that is!).

I think I probably spoke to his GP, from recollection, and they booked an appointment. At that point, I didn't have Power of Attorney for my dad, so the information I could be given from them was limited. It's the one thing I would heartily encourage anyone with elderly parents to do as early as possible, so you can assist, and act legally for them if you ever need to. It can take a while to sort out through the solicitor, and it doesn't mean you have to take instant total control of that person - you work together to make appropriate decisions.

We arrived at the car park of the Mulberry Centre, and I was really hoping that they wouldn't find anything, but at the same time I wanted to know if there was anything that could explain what had happened, and if he needed help.

I sat in with him, as the specialist conducted a multitude of tests. I really felt for Dad as it can't have been easy. He normally loved tests and anything to assess his intellect, but I feel sure he wasn't so keen for this one. It wasn't until quite recently I looked through my voice recordings on my phone, and I realised I still had a recording of the test. It was a surprise to hear his voice again, even under such circumstances.

He did really well, a few memory slip ups, but nothing of any real note, until towards the end of the test.

He had to give a nonsensical answer to a question. For example, what's the capital of England? Banana. And yet he couldn't, for want of trying, give an answer to any of those types of questions. The assessor tried again and gave examples, nothing. She finished up the test and we walked out together to await the results.

It seemed quite a long wait for the diagnosis, but we went back to see the same lady and she sat us down to explain.

There *was* something that wasn't quite right.

She explained that Dad had something called Frontal Lobe Dementia. She said this was not a common variant, and that it attacked the part of the brain responsible for both logic and reasoning.

Well, how incredibly ironic was that? By some cruel twist of fate, the very thing that my dad prided himself on, was being attacked.

Dad and I sat, trying to take in the enormity of what she had said. As usual, Dad appeared to take it in his stride, not really giving much away. (I think he would have made an excellent poker player, come to think of it).

I don't know about him, but once again, I had a million questions buzzing around in my brain.

What does that mean now? How different will that be from Mum's condition? What can be done to help? Etc., etc.

In the forefront of my mind, I was thinking about what we were going through with Mum, and would this be the same for him? I didn't really want to consider that was even a possibility.

The specialist was ever so kind, and I must admit seemed extremely proactive in comparison to Dad's GP. She was liaising and sending over the diagnosis, so they were fully aware, and also organised Dad's medication that, in the same way as Mum's original medication, might help to slow cognitive decline.

She also mentioned that there was a carer support group, that met regularly and wondered if I'd like to join. On consideration I didn't, but it was a nice to know there was support available if people needed it. I think because I was balancing all the other areas of my life, it just seemed like another thing to manage.

We came out of the centre in deep thought and walked together, back to the car. It reminded me once again of that fateful day after Mum's diagnosis. Pretty depressing to say the least.

I think it was the unknown that preyed on both our minds.

I wanted him to know that I was there for him. I can't recall the exact conversation. I feel sure I made it clear to him that we would all support him, no matter what the issues.

Hopefully he knew that anyway, but I didn't want him

to feel he was on his own.

Dad had always done so much for me growing up, and now also for my growing family, both with his time, skills, and finances.

Over the years he had made a bike from scratch for me, he'd welded and worked on my various old cars, (doing a welding course, so he could fix them). He built our kitchen, he put in electrics, did plumbing, put up pictures, even helped at my gym by doing a health and safety assessment and instigating remedial measures. I could go on.

In the earlier days of mine and Lisa's relationship (when we were 'courting' - I love that old fashioned word), Mum and Dad had helped us out financially when we had struggled to pay all the bills. Then later with four kids, a mortgage, cars, fuel, bills, it all added up and they helped whenever we needed them to.

They'd bought us TVs and fridges, given us their old cars to use, and even helped pay to cover my wages when I was ill with chronic fatigue and I was on statutory sick pay. Again, the list could go on.

I feel blessed that we had a happy, healthy and fun relationship with them, because I know a lot of families that just don't get on as well.

I'm not too sure if it was a knee-jerk reaction to the

actual diagnosis, but Dad did appear to change a little afterwards. Whether it was because his condition was named, and out in the open, or if it was a natural progression of his disease, I don't know, but there appeared a slight decline in his cognitive ability. Or perhaps we were just more aware?

Other family members were informed, and they visited him to offer support. It wasn't openly talked about, but it was good they showed solidarity.

Whether it was denial, or tough mindedness, Dad made the decision to enrol on an Open University course. He had already started one, and was two thirds of the way through. I believe the first one was computer electronics, but this one was mathematics related. (Still quite academic.)

Dad told me he would have loved to have gone to University, but the option wasn't there where he was younger. I think there was a financial reason, but I don't think his parents were that keen.

It was very different from now. It appeared to be only a select few that went on to higher education then, as opposed to a much higher percentage now. I think this was why he chose his career in the RAF, so he could learn on the job, with structure and great career options.

He would have made a very good student, and I feel sure he would have been very capable of a Masters and higher.

Sadly, over time and not for the want of trying, he realised that the Open University was an uphill battle, with his diminished processing and logic, and he quietly put it to one side. That must have been tough realisation.

In terms of Dad's overall health, he still had a number of issues we needed to keep an eye on. To minimise the chance of blood clots, he was still taking Warfarin, and was still getting his INR levels checked twice weekly. (This stands for international normalised ratio, which indicates how long the blood takes to clot.) The local doctors' surgery he was registered at was stopping doing INR testing due to a combination of factors including staffing and budget. We needed to register Dad with a new surgery to continue the testing.

It wasn't until all this was set up, I realised just how much variance there was in the quality and service between surgeries. I assumed they were similar in how they were run - how wrong was I! This one was loads better!

They were better organised, friendlier, way more 'on the ball,' and came across hugely more professional.

Dad tended to see one of the nurses when he went for

his bloods to be checked, and I was pleasantly surprised to see that I knew her. She was a regular triathlete competitor (a very good one), and I knew her from when my kids used to compete too.

She was an absolute star, and I will be forever in her debt. (If you ever read this Celia, I will always be eternally grateful for your kindness, consideration and professionalism.)

She made my life much easier by ensuring Dad's INR levels were in good shape because if they went AWOL, as they sometimes did, it meant increased frequency of testing. I think she knew it was already a tight balancing act getting him to these appointments.

It also helped that she was a dab hand at getting into Dad's veins! (His previous chemotherapy had caused many to collapse).

I have to say it was also a massive task to get Dad to hydrate! I had to pick him up a fair bit earlier than his appointment to ensure he'd drunk something!

The other worrying factor was that he was forgetting which day was which, and what time it was. (Not taking in the outside light cues for morning or evening.) As a consequence, I'd arrive to take him to an appointment, and he was not washed or dressed.

From that point on, if we needed to see Dad to pick

him up, we'd ring in advance to prompt him.

The carers were still coming in for him, but they could only coerce, and not force, so the 'Dollery obstinance' was rearing its head. I guess it was his way of retaining some control over his life, when more and more things were getting out of his grasp.

With the confusion of times and days, I managed to get him an Alzheimer's clock, which helped him to have a reference for am and pm and it could 'speak' times and dates. I also got him a big central diary where he could tear off the corner as the days progressed. It was little things like this that could make a big difference.

Food was still a struggle. As he couldn't drive anymore, I had to take him shopping and therefore I was able to excerpt some influence on what foods made it into the basket! (I have to say though it was always a battle of wills!)

He still ate some of the Wiltshire Farm Foods meals, on top of the additional shopping, so there was some sustenance there. (When he chose to eat it all.)

Up to this point, every so often, Dad had been having the occasional week away, knowing Mum was safe at Holywell, which I heartily embraced.

At this point, he paid for all the trips himself and had

gone on the Lochs and Glens tours of Scotland, which he loved. Everything was organised - pick up, transport, hotels, meals, trips and all with a guide and a coach load of likeminded people.

I thought it was great because everything was done with time and precision, just as he liked, and there seemed to always be a few ladies that took Dad under their wing. It was lovely for someone to make a fuss of him, and it was definitely a distraction from other areas of his life.

I was however starting to get a little bit worried at how he would now cope with his slight decline in everyday function.

As Dad was sitting and lying down more, as we had already seen with Mum, he suffered with some muscle wastage.

As a previous personal trainer, I cannot reinforce enough the importance of keeping moving and using muscles on a regular basis, even with additional support if necessary. This is true for anybody of any age, but especially as we get older.

I was surprised to read that we can start losing muscle through age, from as young as our mid to late twenties. Obviously, movement and strength-based work is key.

A huge issue with a growing population of elders is the increased risk of falling. Some local authorities offer what they call a falls prevention programme and I think it's an incredible, vital service. There are also some other national programmes to encourage movement and strength.

Dad had been offered some help through the GP, where someone came to the house to help with exercise, and set him up on a home programme. Sadly though, as he was not doing his homework, the assistance stopped.

The reason that falling is such a huge issue, is that as our age increases, it can potentially increase the likelihood of shock and trauma to the whole body.

I can remember our elderly neighbour going into hospital for a minor operation, fell out of bed, and died from the trauma of breaking her hip/leg.

Little did I know then, this might be of consequence at a later date.

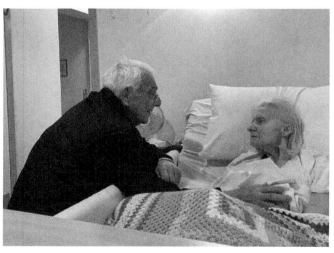

CHAPTER TEN
LISA'S DAD - BO

Unfortunately during this time, we also had another bombshell to deal with.

Lisa was away on a course in London, it was late at night and I heard the landline ring. It woke me up with a start because Lisa had just changed the phone system and I didn't recognise the ring. I was a bit befuddled, as my mum would have said.

It was past midnight, so immediately I thought who could this be? And could only assume it was urgent. It was Lisa's brother, Robert.

I listened carefully, still half asleep, but with a little boost of adrenaline from the sudden waking.

"You need to go round to my mum and dad's. It looks like Dad's had a heart attack. The ambulance is round there with Mum right now!"

Oh! My! That got the adrenaline pumping further.

I threw on some clothes and raced across the road. Luckily, they lived only two houses away. As I walked towards the house, the ambulance was outside, and all the house lights were on. I walked in, anxious about what I might find. I could hear the ambulance crew upstairs, and what sounded like noises of them 'working' on Lisa's dad, Bo. They were doing CPR and had been using the electric shock paddles. I didn't go upstairs - I didn't want to get in the way, so I called up to Sue, Lisa's mum.

She came down, and was obviously in complete shock, wandering around looking in the same places over and over for Bo's medication, when it transpired the ambulance crew already had it.

I tried to settle and comfort her. We hugged and I persuaded her to sit down, encouraging her to tell me what had happened. I held her hand and tried to reassure her, but she was very confused. It must have been the shock.

I did the usual British thing again and put the kettle on to make a cup of tea.

I know for sure with all this chaos, she was so grateful to see a familiar face, but to this day she can't remember me being there, or any of the finer details. Perhaps that was the brain's natural defence mechanism?

Bo had been resuscitated, but was unconscious, and went in the ambulance accompanied by Sue and Lisa's brother Robert, who had now arrived.

I went home to try and come down from all the drama but as you can imagine, that was easier said than done.

I had to let Lisa know. I thought long and hard as to the best way to approach this. She was in London on a course, and it was the middle of the night.

I made an executive decision not to tell her there and then, as she wouldn't have been able to get a train back in the middle of the night, and I felt very sure she would not have slept and then been frustrated at not being able to get home when she wanted.

I texted her early in the morning, saying please contact me urgently and then when I hadn't heard by 7am, I rang her. She knew something was up from the early call.

As soon as I told her what had happened, Lisa got the next train back to Burnham-on-Sea. When she arrived, I picked her up and took her straight to Musgrove Hospital in Taunton.

Little did we realise that we would become more familiar with this place in the future.

After a thorough investigation, the medical team discovered Bo had extensive damage to his body and brain, and we were told it was unlikely he would be able to speak or function as he had done before.

He was 'hooked up' in intensive care and was in an

induced coma. What a shocking sight. The closest family members were all at the hospital, and other family members were made aware.

After being together by his bedside at interspersed periods, we also gathered in the family lounge, which was a separate area kept for close relatives of those with loved ones in critical care.

It had seats, sofas, coffee and tea making facilities and even a little courtyard garden. It was a well needed little sanctuary away from the chaos that was just outside that door.

After all the investigations and explanations, heart wrenching decisions had to be made. It was explained that due to the brain damage, Bo would not be able to feed, walk, or speak.

After discussing the options, a family decision was made to switch off life support. The family agreed that he would not want to live in that state, as he was such a proud, independent and strong man. If he could not function without others' help, he would not want to live.

When they removed life support, we were informed he would not be conscious during this time, and they would let him pass peacefully, but it was not an instant process.

We decided each of us would say our goodbyes to him before life support was switched off and not return.

When both Sue and Lisa said their goodbyes, I lost it. I felt so much for all the family, but especially Lisa, Robert and Sue, and not forgetting all the grandchildren. Such a heart wrenching process.

His life support was switched off on the Thursday, and he was made as comfortable as possible but he didn't pass until Sunday afternoon.

Lisa actually had a dream which suggested he had passed. Her sleep patterns were, understandably, all over the place, and she had fallen asleep on that Sunday afternoon. The phone ringing woke her up with a start from the dream she felt symbolised his passing away.

We all agreed, not going back to see him was the right thing to do, but because of how many days it was afterwards, Lisa felt incredibly guilty at 'leaving' him. It was extremely painful to sit and watch him, so I can understand why the decision was made. I feel sure Bo would not have wanted anyone to endure watching his death. He was made comfortable with medications and excellent nursing care, but it was still an incredibly difficult situation.

A log was made of every day of his care and it was written with the exact spoken word, as if he was conscious, and there are some wonderful comments in there. Lisa's mum did manage to read it after some time had passed. He had great care.

One amazing thing that did come from this however was that we were able to donate some of his organs to help others. What an amazing gesture.

Bo's corneas and the whites of his eyes, helped an amazing five people to live a more comfortable life.

Unfortunately, because of the time taken once life support was switched off, some organs could not be used, including for one individual who had been prepped and ready for a major organ transplant.

Sue was awarded the certificate and the golden hearts to signify Bo's use of his body parts. It's amazing to think that part of Bo lives on, within someone else.

The funeral was organised at the Sedgemoor Crematorium, and a lot of people came as he was well-known and liked in many circles: the local Courts, as he was a Justice of the Peace, the football community through his involvement with Bath, Minehead, and his spot on the board for Bristol city, and the local clubs.

There was standing room only, and some lovely speeches. Friends and family spoke warmly of a very well-respected and loved man. There was even a last minute speech from one of his best friends, who had unfortunately got stuck in traffic. We all felt for him, but he did incredibly well under the circumstances.

The venue for the wake afterwards was large, as we expected lots of people would come, and we were not wrong.

I took Dad. Our neighbours Debbie and Ian kindly helped take care of him too, supplying him with lots of food from the buffet - I counted three plates!

A few people had noticed Dad's decline and were also asking about Mum.

I distinctly remember one thing from this day - whether it was because he was tired, or it was a dementia development but he exclaimed,

"I need to go to the Toist."

I said sorry Dad, to infer for him to repeat himself and he said,

"Toist! Toist! I need to use the Toist."

I knew what he was getting at - toilet, but he said it with such conviction, as if to say why don't you understand what I'm saying?

Unfortunately, all that food had not agreed with him, and I waited with him as he tried to clean himself up in the men's cubicle. He would not let me help him, so it took rather longer than it should have. Luckily no one else needed this toilet whilst he was sorting himself out.

As the day was coming to a close, and because of how he felt, we took him home.

CHAPTER ELEVEN
ANOTHER FALL

Thank goodness for the carers going in to see Dad. They continued to be our eyes and ears. Lisa and I, becoming more concerned for him, went to see him more frequently. Without the carers, I don't think I would have been able to work half as much.

I actually felt guilty not spending as much time as I wanted with Dad but at the same time, I was running a business, and providing for my family. It was always a guilt trip.

Between all of us, I think we juggled everything effectively.

I had noticed that Dad had declined on various levels - personal hygiene, clothes, food and just life. The meticulous Dad was diminishing.

Despite the walking aids, I think he was genuinely frightened of falling again. He was watching television less, and not even reading. That was the definite clincher for me that something was not right.

He ate, slept and breathed reading. It was a massive part of his life. He loved to learn, but he also liked to lose himself within a book.

He was known to read two to three books every week, and yet now he was just not interested. I was very worried at this new development.

Had his condition worsened so much that reading was harder to process?

A few weeks passed by without too much of a hitch, which was almost a little disconcerting in itself, as we had become accustomed to them.

Well, that was about to change.

A bit of background to Dad's impending fall.

After our son Tom moved from King Alfred's School to Brymore Academy (which unusually was a working farm and partly residential school), he flourished both academically and physically. He loved his sport and had been given the chance to try lots of different ones. There were always activities on, whether it be before, during or after school.

One such activity was athletics, specifically, the javelin.

To cut quite a long story short, Tom went from total

novice, to winning the regionals, and then coming third at the Somerset counties athletics meeting, all in a matter of weeks!

He practiced lots with me, joined Taunton Athletic club, and then after much research and emailing, I managed to get him coached at Loughborough University, where he flourished even further.

In the space of two seasons and many competition wins, he was selected to represent England for his age group!

The reason I mention this, is because he was competing in an international attended by teams from Scotland, Ireland and Wales, all the way up in Grangemouth, Edinburgh.

We had to cut a well needed holiday in Ibiza short, so Tom and I could travel north.

Obviously, I was concerned for Dad, but he seemed fairly stable and with Lisa, Josie, Ella and Liv in Ibiza, and now myself and Tom away from home, I asked Lisa's mum Sue to keep an eye on him.

Tom and I decided to take a road trip, via Alton Towers, and have some fun at the same time. After all, it's quite a drive, nearly the whole length of the UK.

I should have known at that point that we had tempted fate and it wouldn't be plain sailing.

When we got near to the B&B just by Alton Towers, I had a phone call.

It was the carers explaining that Dad had fallen again, this time out of bed, and was on his way to Weston Hospital. He had luckily used his neck pendant and the ambulance had arrived and taken him to get checked out.

Typical! I'm nowhere near him, and Lisa and the kids are abroad. I spoke to the hospital and gave them all the information they needed.

What was I to do?

I called Lisa's mum, who also had her sister Dot staying with her and they so very kindly visited him in hospital, and took him everything he needed, for what was hopefully a short stay.

I was torn. I knew I had to take Tom to his competition, but I was extremely worried for Dad's health. At least we knew he was in the best place.

Between Sue, Dot, Lisa and I, we checked, and were kept regularly updated. He appeared in good spirits despite the fall, and I know he would have appreciated the extra attention, high level of care, and the support of the hospital team.

We found out though, after a lot of checks and tests, that Dad had broken his hip when he fell out of bed.

Oh! No!

This was far more serious than we first thought.

Now, as you now know, in the elderly, this is of particular concern, because it can be a massive trauma to the whole system, especially when someone is already frail.

The next few days were a mixture of concern for Dad, but also nerves for Tom's forthcoming competition. I was trying not to place any further stress on him, but I was extremely worried for Dad's welfare. Lisa and rest of the kids luckily returned home soon after.

It was competition time. Tom had six throws to show his best. He had some good warm up throws which created some confidence.

Javelin, being an extremely technical sport, can be hit or miss, even for the professionals. It looks like you just run up and throw, but when you break it down slowly, there's a lot of consecutive elements, each of which affect the next stage. To produce a good throw, each element must support the next, so it's never easy to produce consistently good throws.

Tom's first few throws were good, but still not quite his best. He had been awarded third seed, based on his personal best and those of the other athletes, so he was a bit cross, that all bar the last throw, he was fourth.

Tom put all his effort into the very last throw and managed to increase his distance and propel himself into bronze medal position!

He was on the podium on his very first international competition!

Tom's podium photos were not all smiles, because he had wanted to do better. (His inner critic at work!) But we were all incredibly proud of him.

Lisa's Mum, Aunty Dot and Lisa's brother Robert had taken the trip up to support him, and they all had their photos taken with Tom for the family album. They flew up one-way, so I drove us all the way back to Somerset, javelins and all in one big trip (with a few toilet breaks).

So, once we were all back home, the focus obviously returned to Dad.

He was in hospital for quite a while, to allow his bones to mend. He'd had a huge operation to fix the break, which was as invasive as a hip replacement, all whilst balancing his bloods and his weak kidneys. Quite a task for a man not at peak health, to say the least.

Conversely, after he felt a little better, post op, he said that he liked all the attention and care he was getting. My mum was always very attentive to him, and it was something he understandably had missed.

After things appeared to be more settled, it was decided

that he go into our local cottage hospital within Burnham-on-Sea. This made it easier to visit him.

Whilst all this was going on, I was still going in to see Mum, but had made the decision not to tell her. I had decided, rightly or wrongly, that it would be confusing or painful or perhaps both.

Sadly, I don't think she would have understood. I reasoned that as Mum didn't recognise us anymore, she was at a stage where it would do more harm than good. I was truly unsure how much she understood of what was going on around her. Whenever I visited I continued to speak to her as if she did understand, just in case. I talked about what I had been up to, the children and Lisa, but I could see no sign whatsoever that anything was getting through. I did feel though, it was important to carry on as normal. Whatever that was now.

Lisa had decided some while ago that the children say their goodbyes prior to their nan declining too far. So, one Sunday, they spent time with her, told her what they wanted her to know, kissed her and said their tearful final goodbyes. Having seen Mum towards the end of her journey, I know it was the right decision. It was important they remember her as she was, and not how she became at the end.

I took photos of Mum throughout, and had obviously got used to the decline because I can remember showing one photo to Lisa's mum, and she gasped out loud when she saw it.

I hadn't even given it a thought, and certainly hadn't meant to shock her, it was just that Sue hadn't seen her for such a long time, and it was a huge contrast to how she remembered her. It made me realise, that I had obviously got used to her decline.

So, Dad was transported very carefully to our local hospital and was given his own room, which was very nice. Regular care and attention were gratefully received once again.

They helped Dad with some physiotherapy, being careful not to instigate any more falls or accidents. It was important for him to become weight bearing once again, and to strengthen the muscles for at least the basic physical movements.

The hospital was very concerned for his aftercare, so questioned me about what was going to happen, when he was ready to leave the hospital.

Obviously he had the carers visiting three times daily, but I was hugely worried now, post-accident and hip-break, about the in-between times.

I had already discussed that I wanted him to take some

respite care at a home, which I knew would be an uphill battle, as he was just looking forward to getting back to his own home. I totally understood that, but would it now be safe enough for him?

I had many conversations with him about my concerns of him falling again, and how it might be nice to get short term care, to ease him back into his own home. He might enjoy not to have to worry about cooking, and how he would be looked after there 24/7. I had already done my research and had found a wonderful residential home, if he chose to agree to my plan.

I felt guilty, once again, going behind his back, but I reasoned it was for his benefit. I had spoken to him about getting a month's care initially, but I was secretly hoping he would want to stay on. I thought at least if he tried it, and liked it, he might see the value.

The Towans was a beautiful Victorian manor house with individual rooms, communal lounges and beautiful gardens, looking out to sea, right on the Burnham beach. On a clear day, you could see over to Minehead and beyond to South Wales.

It had an excellent reputation and the instant I stepped into the building I knew why. I'm a great believer in trusting your 'gut' (there's some very interesting science as to why, but that's another story). I instantly felt good vibes about the place and was made very welcome by the smiley home accounts manager.

I was ushered into one of the lounges that was part of a conservatory, and flooded with lovely natural light. You could see the fluffy white clouds being chased across the blue sky, the manicured gardens and the lovely light sandy beach ahead.

I explained what had gone on to the manager, and provided Dad's medication information, so she knew everything about him and was happy to take him on. I sensed she was a little concerned that perhaps he might have been coerced into it, so I assured her it would be totally his decision.

I think he was on the cusp of what they could cope with though, as it was a residential home, not a care home.

Luckily Dad agreed to receive one month's respite care at the home. I knew he would be in very good hands, so paid the deposit and organised it. I was relieved, to say the least, because I knew that he would be safe for the next month.

I'd consider what would come after, when the time came. I had to take each day as it came, as it was the only way that I could cope mentally. It was a strategy that certainly helped in dealing with Mum's issues, and actually for many parts of my life.

I would heartily recommend this strategy for many aspects of future 'firefighting'. Yes, of course, you do have to plan and think ahead, but sometimes, for your own sanity, it helps just to focus on what's in front of you right now.

One other factor in Dad's care, which I haven't explained in detail, was his unpredictable bowel movements. At his own house, I had previously started to notice that there were 'accidents' happening, not only from the smell, but the mess.

I don't know if it was his dementia, or that he couldn't see as well as he used to, but the bathroom looked like he'd purposely tried to fling it everywhere. Sometimes it was all over the floor, all over the toilet, on the door and even up the wall. As he got undressed and dressed, it spread to the hallway and bedroom, well you can guess the rest.

I think he had tried to clean some of it, but in doing so, had managed to spread it far and wide. Bless him, I know he was aware of it, but I don't think he realised quite how bad it had got.

Previously, he had come to our house and soiled himself, but had put it down to feeling unwell. It was clear something else was not right. We broached the subject, and he agreed to go to the Doctor.

After investigation, it was found he had a bowel prolapse. Crikey, one thing after another, poor Dad.

He had to be extremely careful what he ate, and his absolute favourite meal - curry, was unfortunately off the menu. He had guidance from a nutritionist, had medication to handle the loose stools, and had beefed up nappies. This getting older lark, was not much fun.

So there became another reason in favour of the extra care at the home, but obviously I had to warn the manager. It was all under control, after all the measures, but was something she and the staff needed to be aware of.

When I was initially shown around the home, the manager showed me to the available rooms, and they were all lovely. Beautifully decorated with antique furniture and expensive soft furnishings, they had a lovely 'homely' feel, a real 'home from home'.

I already knew what room would suit Dad, and it was exactly the one Dad chose too, and I knew why. It had the same feel as a room at my nan and grandads, at Pine House Cottage. It felt familiar, welcoming and safe, something he needed right now.

I had agreed with the manager for four weeks of post op recovery, but secretly I hoped that Dad would want to stay on further. Only time would tell.

Obviously, this was Dad's decision but I was torn because it was important to have his best interests at heart too, and given his current mental state, was it right for it to be 100% his decision?

I hated this role reversal, but I had to ensure he was safe and in the best health. I had already spoken to the manager, and asked whether it would be possible for him to stay longer term if he wanted to. She said if he wanted to, he could, and that finances could be arranged linked to selling his house. So, at least I knew it was an option.

He settled in well, and loved all the attention from the staff. He was also happily chatting with some of the other residents in the communal lounges and restaurant. I was so relieved and happy for him.

He liked the food, which obviously had to be adjusted for his nutritional needs and bowels, but he did still have a few 'accidents', which I know embarrassed him.

We visited him more frequently in the first week to make sure he was happy in his new home. There had been so much change these last few months, it had been very tough for him.

Despite seeming happy, he did say he was looking forward to going home, which I understood, but at the same time my heart sank. I tried not to show my emotions but probably didn't hide it well. (I too wore my heart on my sleeve, like my mum).

I wondered whether Dad sensed I would have preferred him to stay on, but whatever the reason, that very night, he put up a bit of a protest and would not get out of his chair to get into bed. The staff could not go against his wishes so there he stayed! (Dollery obstinance!)

CHAPTER TWELVE
THAT NIGHT

Dad had been in the Towans residential home for exactly 10 days when I had a phone call saying that he was not himself, and could they have permission to call the doctor to check up on him, which of course I gave. Both Lisa and I went straight down there.

He appeared very confused, and was talking as if he had regressed to an earlier part of his life.

The doctor said the staff should keep an eye on him, but suggested he might have a urine infection, which would make sense with his current state of mind. Lisa and I stayed with him for quite a while, but he was clearly tired and confused, so we left him to rest. The home said they would keep us updated if anything changed. Later that night, we had another call from Towans to say that Dad had got worse, more confused and he had a temperature now, they felt he needed an ambulance. They were taking him to Musgrove Hospital in Taunton.

Firefighter Dollery, back in action.

We raced down there, extremely worried. He was in an observation bay, which was screened off. We found him, spoke to the staff, and awaited further information. Whilst we were there, Dad did seem rather out of it. He was hallucinating and doing something he loved - eating toast!

He was making all the actions with his arms and hands; taking the bread out of the bread bin, cutting the butter, spreading it, and eating it, and he looked like he was really enjoying it.

This would have been quite bemusing, had it not been in such a worrying context, but he actually looked in a state of bliss. Perhaps the meds had kicked in?

After further observation he was taken into a side ward. They thought he might have an infection from his hip operation, and medicated him appropriately.

The ward didn't have a nice feel to it. There were others there with similar conditions, but worse. It reminded me of my own overnight hospital stay where I was put in the geriatric ward. Throughout the night there were distressed and confused patients wandering and shouting. Unpleasant to say the very least.

I think the thing that concerned me was the staff had looked at Dad's notes and had seen dementia, but they didn't really know how bad it was. He was worse than I'd ever noticed, speaking gobbledegook, and certainly wasn't the dad I knew.

I spoke to a member of staff to relay my concern. They thought it was the infection causing his overall changed demeanour, but I was even more concerned. Even on his worst day, I had never seen him like this.

After a number of stable days, there was a worrying turn of events. They thought he might have an infection within his wound from his hip surgery and they would have to open it up to check and clean it out. Not ideal with somebody so frail, and it would also mean more rehabilitation all over again.

I was taken into a side office and the surgeon explained the risks.

He highlighted the fact there was a chance he might not be strong enough to pull through post op, as he was very frail, but in my eyes he couldn't carry on like this, something *had* to be done.

As if to signify the seriousness of this, they said if I needed to say anything to him, say it now, because they were rushing him straight to surgery.

What do you say to your father who helped to bring you into this world? He had done so much for me over the years, and this might just be the very last thing I say to him?

"I love you Dad, thank you for all you've done, be strong and pull through," and I kissed him on his cheek as the staff rushed him off.

I wasn't sure how much of this he heard or understood because he was so very delirious.

When they opened up his previous wound, there wasn't any infection there, which was totally perplexing. They took blood tests to see if they could indicate anything else.

When the results came back though, it confirmed that what he actually had was Sepsis.

Oh God!

At the time I didn't know much about it, but I knew enough to know it was very serious.

Dad was put in intensive care and monitored, and we stayed with him as he mostly slept and recovered from the trauma of yet another invasive operation. He was at least stable, but not out of the woods yet.

We fed back to family members and my mum's younger brother Ian and his wife Sal came down to support us, and to see Dad. Families can pull together at times like these, and we were extremely grateful for ours.

We stayed with Dad for ages, but as he was mostly sleeping and recovering, Lisa and I (emotionally exhausted by this point) decided to go home and try to get some rest.

The doctors had plied Dad with drugs to aid his recovery, and to ensure he was not in any pain or discomfort, so there wasn't really much for us to do.

We actually hadn't been home for that long, and we got a phone call from the doctor assigned to Dad's case.

He had looked through his case notes and obviously knew all about Dad, but asked me further questions about his home life.

He asked what Dad had generally been like previously, compared to how he was now. He wanted me to make an honest assessment, as to what had transpired previously to this day.

I explained that Dad had been declining steadily, and that he wasn't his usual self. I explained he had lost interest in reading and TV, and about him being in bed, not moving, the falls, and about his personal hygiene, etc.

When you start to collate it all like that, it didn't paint a great picture, poor Dad. I felt he was giving up already, but we had persevered, as you would, and tried to help as much as we could.

Well, he floored me then, because he said that he was not a well man, (which of course we knew) but his kidney function had declined further to such a stage that he would now need regular dialysis, and he didn't think he was strong enough to cope with the regular demands of the treatment.

He felt his quality of life wasn't great, and let me know that the drugs he was currently on, were basically keeping him alive. The Sepsis had really taken hold, and made him gravely ill.

What he was suggesting, was to take the drugs away, give him pain killers and let him die peacefully.

I felt sick. Oh God, this was it. I knew he was weak and unwell, but in my own mind I didn't think this would be his time to go.

All the while we were firefighting and dealing with individual issues, I still thought in the back of my mind that this was just another thing to deal with, and then we would get back to some normality. It hadn't crossed my mind, until that point, that this was in fact, it.

If I'd have been a betting man, I'd have said, without a shadow of a doubt that Dad would have outlived Mum, and yet here we were - he had hours to live, and Mum, who can't move, speak or do anything for herself, in a body of skin and bones, soldiers on.

We went straight back to spend time with him, and we let Ian and Sal know the sad news.

Dad was put in a quiet private side ward, where he was assigned a lovely end of life nurse, and we were all able to spend quality time with him.

When he came round, he was able to comprehend some of our talk and respond, albeit quietly and slowly. It was incredibly moving.

As you might imagine I was a mess, and I think Dad was surprised to see me so emotional and crying. He looked perplexed.

I made the decision that he shouldn't know he was dying. Rightly or wrongly. He was relaxed and appeared so peaceful. I did wonder what he would have been like if he knew, but I felt it fairer for him not to.

It made me think of my childhood and growing up. I had a million images going through my head, family holidays, memorable moments, growing up, and all the time we spent together. I cried lots more.

We all reminisced about old times and talked together, Lisa and I, my uncle and aunt, and Dad. He dozed in and out of sleep and then was able to answer some of our questions, amazingly.

In typical 'Dad' style, he had even apologised for causing us all this trouble and worry. Even in his dying moments, he was being considerate to others.

He was resting in a heated air blanket and he looked very cosy and warm. He'd have loved one of these for everyday use, his greatly reduced kidney function meant he really felt the cold a lot of the time.

It reminded me of the time when his gas fire had packed up, unbeknown to us, and I'd come in to find the oven on, with the door left open to try and get some warmth.

Thinking back, it was very peaceful and serene. Away from the hustle and bustle of the rest of hospital and I really appreciated Ian, Sal and Lisa being there for support, it made everything a little easier.

I have to admit though, every time Dad slept, I watched his mouth and his chest rise and fall, wondering if that was his last breath.

We were all drained, understandably, and we took it in turns to watch Dad. I kept falling asleep - the surroundings didn't help, being so warm and quiet. The nurse said to me that they had a bed in the hospital that I could use. I was really reticent, but Lisa said go on, you need at least *some* sleep. I got the key, walked out into the cold dusky night, across the courtyard and to the accommodation. I opened the door and it reminded me of my old college bedrooms - basic, but welcoming.

I had just got undressed, lifted the cover and sheet to get in, and there was a phone call.

"I think you should come back. I'm sorry to say your father has passed'.

I had to process that for a moment. My dad had

passed.

Oh wow, how typical was that?! The moment I go, he does too.

When I've mentioned this to others, they have said it happened for a reason, and that he didn't want me to be there when he went. Perhaps that was so. If that was indeed his wish, then I'm happy it happened that way.

I think at this time we were all shell shocked. I did say my goodbyes but I purposely didn't stick around for long.

The rest of the day, after sleep, was a bit of blur. I remember waking up with the realisation that he *had* actually gone.

I found it incredibly hard to go back to his house and see all his personal belongings. His shoes, his glasses, items of favourite clothing, as they all had memories and emotions attached to them. I found it strange that I would never physically see him again. I had a good cry to grieve, and let it all out. It had been a hell of a journey for Dad too, over these last few years.

There was an awful lot of sorting out to do. It made me realise that with Dad gone, and Mum in her care home, their home was now empty, and it was my responsibility to sort it all out. It certainly wasn't empty of *stuff*, but soulless - just like my grandparents' house had been when they passed. It had only been three months since Lisa's Dad, Bo had died, so it was a lot to take in.

I cried a bit more there, composed myself and then locked up, deciding to save tackling all that for another day.

With the reality of Dad's death, we suddenly had to think of long-term care for Henry the cat. We had been in to see him and feed him, but now he needed a more permanent home. We decided we would look after him, after all he was the link between Mum, Dad and I.

At the time we already had three cats and a dog; Murphy the Maine Coon, Dizzee the British shorthair and Mac the Persian, together with Leo the Labrador. Henry was obviously used to being by himself, so it was quite a change for him. Let's just say he didn't like it one bit. We tried lots of different tactics, but after we got him used to the inside of our house, every time he went out, he went back straight to the old house. We counted that he did this a dozen times, and that was more than a mile away across a very busy road. Each time we went back to call and find him.

To cut a very long story short, after looking at every opportunity, my mum and dad's neighbour Chris agreed to take him in. I was so grateful, as it meant he was safe, happy and in an area he knew well. I do see him occasionally when I pass by Mum and Dad's old place.

CHAPTER THIRTEEN
THE FUNERAL

Dad's death made me realise there was an awful lot to sort out. I'd never organised a funeral before, I Googled it to create a list, so I could tackle all the necessary points.

I contacted all my clients at Personal Space gym, who were very understanding when I said I needed to take a couple of weeks off to sort everything out. I don't think my head would have been sufficiently 'in the game' to function effectively anyway.

I still had to keep an eye on Mum, but obviously she was in good hands at Holywell. Somehow with Dad gone, I suddenly felt a lot more responsibility for her. The onus was all on me now.

Despite being in full time care, I was now in sole charge of her welfare and making all the decisions relating to her.

I realised that despite Dad's poor health, he had still

shielded me in some way, as the home had still gone through him for decisions and questions. That protection, no matter how small it was, had now gone.

The list of tasks for the funeral seemed long, but I knew I just had to take each day as it came, and get done what I could, when I could. Having never done this before, it was all new territory, but I wanted to do the very best for him that I could, in his honour.

I love making lists as it makes me feel more organised. I do it the old-fashioned way with pen and paper, and derive great satisfaction from scoring through or ticking off items – sometimes even both!

I set to work, compiling a list for the funeral, which was the priority, but secondary to that, the mammoth task of all the 'house stuff' which needed to be done.

As Dad's case had been complicated the coroner was involved, so I had to speak to the coroner's office to get an interim death certificate. They were very efficient, polite and professional, but basically his death had to be fully investigated and an official report produced into the cause of death. It took quite a while, but eventually the official cause of death listed on his certificate was Sepsis.

I had to register his death with the local registry office, and obtain printed copies of his death certificate, so I could sort all his paperwork and financial affairs. I was amazed how many companies required a death certificate as proof of death rather than just taking my word for it!

I knew this was going to be a significant task!

I think we've already established that Dad didn't like to get rid of anything. Nothing. Nada. There was going to be an awful lot to sort out.

I had approached 'decluttering' with him by saying, "Why don't we just try and empty a box a week?" But just as the clearance of Spider Cottage had been an uphill struggle, this one was a total road block! (Dollery Obstinance?)

Luckily, I found an address book in the house and spread the sad news of Dad's passing.

Mum, having been an avid letter writer, had kept it fairly up-to-date, when she was able to, and luckily I didn't have to call each of them with the sad news, as one person after another agreed to ring round others on my behalf.

I started to look through paperwork to try and find details on all Dad's financials, and knew it was going to be quite a task. There were boxes and boxes and piles of papers, all over the house. However, in reality, it was actually way worse than I had originally thought it might be.

One thing Dad did tell me though, when he was lucid, was that he kept all his important things in a silver box. I knew where that was, as he'd shown me - it was in his bedside cabinet drawer. Alongside it were some Werthers originals, keys, copious notes, model aircraft, Christmas cracker toys and a multitude of other not particularly useful things!

Looking through the box it became apparent this was more like a trinket box, however whilst it had things like his RAF registration, some old wage slips, and notes, it had nothing of real importance, like his will, life insurance, funeral plan details, etc.

Where to look next?

I tackled the piles of papers that were on show, then the ones inside the filing cabinet and finally, the readily available boxes that weren't in the loft.

I was very careful sifting through all the papers, as I didn't want to miss anything, but at the same time I needed to get rid of unimportant things and clear some space too - I didn't want to just move stuff around.

After a fair bit of searching, Lisa and I found a funeral plan, in fact two! I think Dad had forgotten about the first and organised another, certainly a lot better than none at all!

Bless him, he was always so considerate and thought ahead to ensure the money was available and the plan was in place to make things easier.

I contacted the company, let them know what had happened and filled out all the paperwork - which was a ridiculous amount and had to be checked with a fine tooth comb, to ensure it was above board and official.

Lisa's father's recent funeral had been handled by a local independent funeral director, who were absolutely amazing. They were extremely professional, courteous, and for an event so emotionally charged, dealt with everything with dignity.

I felt I'd prefer to use them, rather than the national Co-operative Dad had organised. After paying a small admin fee, luckily I was able to access funds to go with R.Millard and Son, the local option.

I arranged an appointment, and talked through what I wanted. They helped organise other aspects such as a newspaper notification, order of service printing, and all associated paperwork, which really helped to relieve the pressure.

I had to think about how Dad's body would be transported, the overall number of mourners for the cars, where to hold the ceremony, a venue for the wake, where he was to be buried, and who was leading the ceremony.

There was only one stipulation that I could find from Dad's funeral plan, and that was to be categorically, absolutely sure he was dead before we buried him!

He had explained once that he'd had a recurring nightmare of being trapped in a coffin, and being buried alive, and he certainly didn't want to go through that! Crikey! Definitely not! Apparently it's a common fear.

I felt I had enough knowledge to organise a funeral that would suit him. It had to be just right.

In a way, despite the responsibility being all mine, at least it was my decision, and I could do exactly as I thought best, without having to answer to others or compromise on things I thought were important.

With the core funeral aspects addressed, I organised the flowers, spoke to the wake venue regarding catering and approximate numbers, and started writing the service, choosing the music, and writing the eulogy.

I chose the same venue for Dad's funeral service as Lisa's family had chosen for her father - Sedgemoor Crematorium. It was a lovely venue, (if that's the right word) with plenty of parking. It was easy to find, and was close to both the burial plot and venue for the wake.

I did check that Lisa and Sue were ok with that, as I was worried it might upset them, seeing as we were all here so recently for her dad.

I went to the Windmill Inn Club to discuss food options for the wake, and we thought the best thing was to sample some food before making our decision.

Whilst we were there, they had a carvery, which was excellent.

Originally, I had envisaged a finger buffet, but they are always quite 'beige' looking, as Lisa and I call it - sausage rolls, bread rolls, crisps etc., nothing too inspiring.

The manager told me the prices per head, but at the same time I noticed the carvery price was very similar.

Dad loved a good carvery!

A carvery was much nicer and I thought as people would be travelling from far and wide they would appreciate something more substantial than a few sausage rolls! (My nan would have approved!)

So, we ate there, enjoyed it, and booked the carvery for approximate numbers, including self-service tea and coffee. Perfect and fitting!

I had started putting an order of service together, including hymns and music. The chosen pastor was a lovely lady and had such a gentle way about her. She instantly put me at ease and offered full support and guidance as to what to expect on the day. She gave me a framework for the eulogy, and I started noting all my personal details within it.

Out of everyone who knew about Dad's death, nobody had come forward to say they wanted to say something at the funeral. I had deliberated and deliberated about whether I should speak. Lisa felt I would be too emotional, and I wondered whether I could do it?

I wrote the eulogy, but also wrote a separate piece about my dad that I asked Marion the pastor to read on my behalf. It's something I regret not reading myself now, but I felt at least my sentiments were known, and I was able to convey my feelings through her.

Obviously writing that was very emotional. It was imperative that I make Dad proud, but it was the music choice that got me.

Anyone who knows me well will tell you I adore my music. It means such a lot to me, and I couldn't live without it. The thing is, I *feel* the music - it speaks to me and gets me physically. I often get shivers, or tingles or even goosebumps from pieces of music.

Dad enjoyed his music too and on reflection he had quite discerning tastes. It was fairly straightforward to get a list, because I'd made a playlist for Dad's 'epic day out in the Spitfire', the problem was narrowing it down!

What music would suit Dad, suit the moment, and sum him up?

I chose a piece by Pink Floyd for the coffin entering the building – 'Shine on You Crazy Diamond'. It fitted. Even one of the funeral staff commented, "What a great track." I'm listening to it right now, with tears in my eyes.

I also chose 'Breathe' by Pink Floyd for reflection. It was only just under 3 minutes, so not that long, but long enough to reflect and it was a track he'd played often.

I wanted to include an RAF-related song and managed to find a medley which included many of Dad's favourite film themes - The Dam Busters, Reach for the Sky, etc. which played as he left the crematorium. Yes, I felt it was very fitting. I feel sure Dad would have approved.

I gave the full order of service to Millard's, along with the eulogy and the, 'What I learnt from my Dad.' piece to Marion the pastor.

Everything was starting to come together and I was looking forward to it in a way, but just to get through it successfully.

There's no malice in that statement whatsoever, I just wanted it to go right, be befitting, and I think get a sense of closure, relief from the last few turbulent months.

That day came soon enough.

I woke up that morning and instantly felt the butterflies in the pit of my stomach. This was indeed the day.

I washed and shaved being very careful not cut myself for the awaiting white shirt, and got my newly purchased black suit. I had already buffed my black shoes to a pleasing shine.

Lisa, all the kids and I looked incredibly smart and I have no doubt Dad would have approved of our presentation. I know some funerals are more casual these days, but to me it's a mark of respect to be smart and I knew Dad would have wanted it that way.

The butterflies in my tummy turned from small Whites, to huge Red Admirals, in a matter of seconds when I saw Dad's funeral car, and the procession behind. All the funeral staff looked incredibly smart and respectful.

Ok then, here we go.

The cars went slowly to the venue, and I could see people slowing down to respectfully allow the cortége to pass. I tried to focus ahead, and stay composed, but it was an intense inner battle. Such huge emotions.

As we arrived at the venue, I could see quite a few family members and friends had already gathered. I managed to greet a number of them without being too wobbly, but the start of the music for Dad to enter the crematorium set me off, just a little.

We had already been told what we needed to do to carry my dad. So, my Uncle Ian, Tom my son, one of the staff from the funeral director and I listened carefully again to the instructions.

We carefully rested Dad down on the plinth and took up our positions in the pews.

Marion read the eulogy and the towards the end of the service read the piece I'd written for Dad. It went like this;

My dad and what he taught me.

My father was a 'gentle-man', in every sense of the word, it was something I was told repeatedly, from many different sources, from those that met him.

Perhaps it was because gentlemen are few are far between these days, but whatever the reason, he personified this.

He was a very polite and courteous man, meant no ill to anyone, and was forthright, upstanding, quiet and unassuming. Kindness shone from his eyes.

My dad helped me throughout my life, always in a very practical way. In my early years he knew I wanted a bike, so he made one, from scratch!

If I needed help with homework, which in the case of maths and physics was lots, he was there.

Before I could drive, he bought me my first car, a classic mini and typical of minis of that age, Dad needed to tackle the inevitable rust. He went to night school, learned how to weld, and went ahead and fixed it!

When Lisa and I moved house, Dad built our new

kitchen. I could go on.

I admit it's a shame his handy skills and practicality didn't rub off on me, but you can't have everything!

He loved the English language, and the use of big words. I think my enjoyment of writing, is matched only by his love of reading.

Where one person might be sleepy, he would be soporific,

Where one might be feeling full, he was satiated,

If he exclaimed enjoyment, it would be to his delectation!

I think you get the idea!

It was my dad who taught me marriage was for life, perhaps this is the reason I might have taken so long to decide (sorry Lisa!).

To his core, he was loyal to my mum, a trait I hold dear to my heart.

In sickness and in health, cannot be any more clearly portrayed, than his love and devotion in caring for my mum, throughout her battle with Alzheimer's.

It seems incredulous that she outlives him today, having just celebrated 57 years of marriage.

Despite very hard times, and poor health, and seeing his dear wife become a shadow of her former self, he stuck by her. Sadly, the person he married no longer recognised him, which unsurprisingly, broke his heart.

One thing my dad maintained, through all the tough years, was a positive mental attitude. When he was diagnosed with cancer the first time, (there were a further two times), he assured me personally, he was going to recover.

He had total conviction in what he was saying, which when you consider he was given 6 weeks to live over 30 years ago, he did pretty well!

Even through all the hardships, he kept positive, which showed just how strong he really was. We soon realised how tough he was, when my mum came to stay, just as her Alzheimer's was gaining foothold. We were exhausted after two days, my dad lived this for 7 years.

My father always put others before himself. Even at his weakest, he was more concerned with the impact his illness was having on those around him, than he was for himself - he didn't want to negatively impact others' lives.

Before my dad died, I conducted a short interview with him, for my own work. I asked him, what his most valuable life lesson was, and he said, "Enjoy. Every. Moment."

Nothing illustrates this more than the picture you see on the cover of your service sheet. I often wondered what more he might have done, had he not had to dedicate his later life to caring for my mum.

My dad taught me to work hard. He was a provider, and he wanted to create a comfortable lifestyle for my mum and I. He rarely rested and was always doing jobs outside his normal day job. My mum also helped by setting the list of jobs to be done!

Another thing he had in abundance was brains! He had a brain that loved to problem solve, which was perfectly suited to his career. This however proved ironic, when you consider he was diagnosed with frontal lobe dementia, which attacked the beloved logic he prided himself on.

Just to prove to himself he could do it, he went to London and took the MENSA test. Based on his high IQ score, he passed and joined. He needn't have, we knew already. I'm still hoping to this day that enough of his brainy DNA has rubbed off on all of us!

So, in closing, I want to say it's been a pleasure and an honour knowing you, Dad.

Despite occasional periods of the 'Dollery obstinance', I'd certainly put up with that, just to spend another day with you putting the world to rights.

They say you don't realise what you have, until it's gone. That is so true.

I love you Dad, and sign off, as you did with the majority of your phone calls to me-

'God bless.'

We gathered around the coffin, all four bearers again, gave our respects, and lifted the coffin back to the car, ready to take him to his final resting place in Berrow, not too far from where he had been living. Music from The Dam Busters and Reach for the Sky blared out over the crematorium speakers including a wartime firefight with explosions and gunfire. (I'd forgotten that was added on!)

I had organised a double grave to be built so that Mum would share the space afterwards, not that I really wanted to consider that, right at that moment. I'd have bet any money Mum would have been the first to go.

For the last time, we carried Dad out of the hearse, to his final resting place.

The graveyard was a beautiful setting, surrounded by fields, sweeping trees and peaceful countryside.

It was family members only by the graveside, and as Marion spoke, we scattered some earth together with some flowers, and said our final emotional goodbyes.

I felt for Lisa and her mum because Bo laid only feet from my dad's grave, a stark reminder of what had happened only weeks before.

The meal at the wake went well, and I know everyone enjoyed the roast dinner. I had quite a lot of feedback about how lovely the service was and how fitting it was for him, which is exactly what I'd hoped.

We had put together a photo album of Dad over the years, for people to look at, and as friends and family flicked through its pages they reminisced, and shared many stories about time they had spent with Dad.

As we said our goodbyes I was starting to feel exhausted. Today had been the culmination of so much work over the last few weeks and based on the feedback, I felt I had achieved what I set out to do. It had been fitting, and had gone as well as these things can.

CHAPTER FOURTEEN
HOUSE CLEARANCE

As you can only imagine, approximately 60 years of accumulated stuff is going to take a fair bit of sorting out.

Where do we even start?

Lisa and I started by attacking some of the paperwork, and this was exactly the right word, as this felt like a military mission!

We needed to sift through the important paperwork and get rid of all the not so important paperwork. Despite the neat-ish piles, there was no order within.

Financial Times, wine lists, sudoku books, BBC History magazine, Lochs and Glens, Red Cross, Fly Past, Donkey Sanctuary, local free-ads, bank statements, The Mail on Sunday, you get the picture?

There was an awful amount of unopened mail as well, which we both had to open and check. I don't know why, but it felt invasive; it needed to be done though to ensure nothing important was missed.

What we were primarily looking for was the power of attorney for Mum, both wills, and all the house bills and bank statements to assess who needed to be contacted, to ensure they knew of Dad's passing.

Being an only child, I felt a huge weight of responsibility to ensure that the house and Mum were safe, and that all the financials were in order.

With Mum still alive (if you could call it that), I felt a pang of guilt sifting through their private affairs.

I still left the heating and water on, but at a low level to ensure the house was still being warmed. I also searched and paid for house insurance, to cover an empty house, I couldn't risk anything going wrong and not being covered.

I knew I still had to pay for Mum's care and was wondering how that was going to work. I did manage to get some cash out of Dad's account before it was closed, to pay for some of it, then the home agreed it could be accrued, whilst I tried to sort everything out.

I assumed it would be frowned upon legally for me to get funds out, but I was desperate to ensure Mum's care was paid for.

Now Dad had gone, I was in sole charge of Mum, so I needed to find the power of attorney paperwork. This would mean in the state's eyes, I could make decisions on her behalf and deal with the estate.

Well, that was certainly easier said than done. We had to dig much deeper than the piles, the filing cabinet and the obvious boxes that were on show.

This was such a laborious process because there was no point just pushing it to another pile, it had to be sorted and dealt with.

It soon became obvious the filing cabinet was not the 'treasure trove' it should have been, as it was mostly Dad's health and safety business files and work, but one major exciting find was the house deeds and associated paperwork.

If I said it took ages, then that would be an understatement. We were tackling this job in our 'spare time' which made it heavy going.

Finally, we found some paperwork relating to Mum's power of attorney, and there was my signature alongside Uncle Ian's. Good find. There was however another power of attorney document alongside it with only Dad's signature. Weird.

After trying to figure out what was going on, we realised there was only one official Power of Attorney and it applied to Dad alone, so was obviously useless.

Oh dear, why is nothing ever easy?

It transpired that Dad had experienced some difficulty

with the original paperwork and because of this, rather than chase myself and my uncle again to sign it, he'd sorted it on his own.

Damn it! Or something much stronger, which I won't write.

One thing was certain, I needed to organise another Power of Attorney for Mum, pronto.

In the eyes of the law, I would need this to make any legal decisions Mum was too incapacitated to make for herself.

I researched local law firms and spoke to one solicitor to get help. I explained what had happened to both Mum and Dad and she listened intently, making notes as we went along. She also gave me some homework, a number of things to both find, and action.

I gave her the house deeds for safe keeping and she already checked and found that the house was in both of their names. Apparently, this made taxation more favourable as it took advantage of each individual tax allowance.

She also explained that as Dad's Power of Attorney was null and void with his passing, we actually needed a higher level for Mum, which we needed to obtain through the courts. Mum had already been assessed by the home to ascertain her level of comprehension, and as you would expect it was pretty much non-existent.

What we needed was a 'Court of Protection' order, which basically meant more expense and a longer process, but it would mean I had the ability to make informed decisions on Mum's behalf.

It would also mean keeping a record of all expenses and reviewing these annually. I agreed this needed to be done, so the solicitor got the ball rolling.

I did find it painful to go back to Mum and Dad's house. It was a stark reminder of what was happening. Despite the important paperwork search, I did procrastinate a little bit on the actual clearing.

We had moved many, many times through Dad's career, so I guess I didn't have any particular affinity to this house, but it was still tough. I think if I had lived there too, and they'd lived longer, I might have felt different.

Whilst it was a lovely house, I would say that for the period of time they owned it, it wasn't particularly the happiest of times, especially compared to other houses and periods of life, but despite this, there were still some good memories.

Whilst my solicitor was sorting the deputyship from the Court of Protection, Mum was continuing her slow decline. She had more frequent chest infections, but each time she received antibiotics, she once again improved.

In my head, I had assumed that with their 'duty of care' for Mum, the home was obliged to prescribe and administer medications, as they saw fit. I must admit, since having sole charge of Mum's care, and dealing with Dad's passing, I hadn't really processed exactly what this meant.

One of the matrons took me to one side and said she needed to have a quiet word. I wondered what she was going to tell me.

She said she realised how much I loved Mum and wanted to be with her, but she was concerned that the antibiotics were just prolonging her suffering. She was obviously well cared for, and her life was made as comfortable as possible, but they wondered whether it was the right thing to do?

I must admit to instantly feeling a huge pang of guilt. Perhaps it was my Catholic school upbringing? (Penance = 25 rosary beads and some Hail Marys, I think).

I honestly hadn't considered it was *my choice* in my new role as Mum's sole guardian. Of course, I said, I do agree, wholeheartedly.

This decision needed to be a collective decision, not just mine. Despite the fact I had verbally agreed it, it had to be jointly agreed by all concerned and transcribed.

Matron helped organise a meeting the following week, where a Holywell Home manager, a matron, Mum's assigned social worker, her G.P. and me, documented fully, her new care plan. I was a little apprehensive with all the authority there, but they were all there with Mum's best interests at heart.

Each person explained where Mum was in her life journey, what had happened to her, her overall condition and what she was now capable of doing. (Sadly, pretty much nothing).

Collectively, it was decided she should not take antibiotics, but also that her 'do not resuscitate' paperwork was updated. This meant if she got an infection, they would only administer medication to make her comfortable, and if she had a heart attack or similar CPR would not be administered.

It doesn't bear thinking about. Can you imagine the physical damage CPR could cause, especially in her frail state, not to mention how confusing that would be for her?

I knew this was the right and necessary course of action.

As we left the meeting, one of the managers who had always been so kind and caring, gave me a huge hug. I welled up, but managed to keep relatively composed. Just.

They really did care, and to me this act confirmed it.

The solicitor was making some progress with the deputyship, and Lisa and I were still ploughing through all the paperwork at the house.

I needed to find all the paperwork related to the house and ensure all was in order. I had closed the bank accounts, and they were frozen, which meant direct debits were not paid. It was imperative that I continued to contact all the companies concerned, to let them know of Dad's passing and the situation.

I listed everything I could find: magazine subscriptions, newspapers, utilities, insurances, local authorities, credit cards, charities, Aster warning pendant, phone, WiFi, etc.

Both Lisa and I informed each one and marked on our lists, whether they required the proof of death certificate and what the outstanding actions were. We both called and emailed, depending on the best contact details we found.

One interesting one was the wine club. Dad in his infinite wisdom had decided to join a wine club, great in itself, but this meant that a case of wine was delivered to his house every month, ad infinitum!

I had wondered why he was accumulating all this wine!

The thing that really got me mad (and that took a lot),

was that because of Dad's medication he couldn't drink anyway. He knew that. I believe he had been coerced into signing up by the telephone marketers. There were a few times when I'd come to his house, and he was on the phone clearly being pressured into something he was unsure about.

When we were finally allowed access to his bank accounts, which listed all the standing orders and direct debits there was a total of over £600 a month, going out on charity donations, magazine/papers subscriptions, and the like.

I wondered how much of this Dad actually wanted, I was beginning to think only a small percentage.

Red Cross, Donkey Sanctuary, Greenpeace, People's Postcode Lottery, Financial Times, BBC History, Money Weekly, Sudoku puzzles, the list went on and on, and the majority were left in their wrappers, just piling up. Whilst Dad was generous to a fault, and was very happy to support multiple charities, it had made me ponder how many he had been coerced into as opposed to willingly signed up to. I do feel there needs to be a closer look at this from a regulatory point of view.

I have to say also that it wasn't easy trying to close these accounts either, some contact details were very hard to find. Was this done on purpose?

My uncles and aunts, realising the enormity of clearing Mum and Dad's house, offered to give two weekends of their time to help. We earmarked two separate weekends and booked huge skips; we also had some very kind friends that offered their assistance too.

I felt so lucky to have this help, it made the enormity of said task a bit more bearable, and it meant the emotional side of things was also somehow shared.

Luckily, I also had a van to take stuff that was too good to throw away to the charity shops. Things felt like they were moving in the right direction.

During this time, I had been called to Holywell twice when Mum had a chest infection. She was extremely poorly, had struggled to breathe and was wheezing and coughing. I really thought the worst could happen, as now there were no antibiotics available.

I seemed to always prepare myself for the worst, and then by some miracle she would pull through. Is this even fair?

How does this happen with someone who is so frail? I really don't know how it's possible. At these later stages Mum was close to weighing only 30kg.

I continued to go to see Mum, freshen the flowers, feed her, speak to her and fill her in on what we had been doing, play music and just be with her.

Despite her not knowing who I was, or being able to engage, I felt comforted just by being with her. Often I just sat and held her hand and laid my head close to hers. She loved to have her face massaged with moisturiser, and it was nice for me to do it for her.

The time had come to get together to clear Mum and Dad's last residence, 7 Braithwaite Place. I'd ordered a 10-yard skip, and had my van on standby to do the charity shop run.

My dad's old bedroom, which I had already cleared, was where I'd asked everyone to put valuable stuff - important papers, personal or sentimental objects, etc.

I'd already done a big shop for sandwiches, biscuits, fruit and copious amounts of tea and coffee, and our lovely friends Pete and Hayley had joined ranks to help.

We divided ourselves initially into areas, so we didn't get under each other's feet; the garage, the loft, the lounge, and the shed.

The garage was full to the ceiling with boxes.

When Mum and Dad moved from Spider Cottage, they not only had all their accumulated stuff, but a lot of my nan and grandad's stuff too.

After they died, and the relatives took what they

wanted, the rest, rather than be given away or dealt with, was stockpiled. Both Ian and Michael (Mum's brothers) dealt with the garage first, as they felt there might be something of interest to them in there. I had obviously said to all relatives, please just take what you want.

Luckily, they found some stuff they wanted, that had been missed the first time around. They put it in their own cars out of the way.

The loft was another area totally filled up with boxes, and other than the obligatory Christmas tree and decorations, I didn't really know what we'd find, only that there would be stuff dating back from many years.

I brought down some extremely heavy and cumbersome boxes for my aunts, Lisa, Sue and Hayley to sort in the lounge, which had now become the central sorting office!

The house was probably more alive now, than it ever had been.

Despite the sombre nature of the process, there was actually lots of hilarity. We reminisced over found objects and photographs which aroused strong and happy memories, and there was lots of chatter and general busying. We were making progress.

The skip was filling up, as was my van with charity donations. Dad's old bedroom was refilling, albeit only with a few sentimental items.

I still find it weird how objects can evoke such strong emotions and how they make you feel, perhaps this is why Dad didn't want to get rid of anything?

We stopped for lunch and all sat in the conservatory, eating, drinking and looking through more old photos we had found. It felt lovely to have the support and kinship, through what had been quite a rough ride.

Once we had eaten, we ploughed through our allotted areas, bringing more boxes down from the loft, trying to unstack the garage boxes and feeding the skip.

We found lots of RAF-related memorabilia, electronic items that looked very dated now, Dad's old computer that he built, and stuff dating back through many decades.

I was interested to see a box full of items relating to Mum and Dad's wedding day, that I'd never seen. Cards, dried flowers, and trinkets from over 50 years ago, the pictures showed such a joyous day. They had lived many happy years after that, so it was important to remember those, as opposed to the turbulent last seven or so years.

I think when you do a huge clear out like this you have to be ruthless because quite honestly, where are you going to put it all?

I did keep some items, but I thought if I keep more, they'll just gather dust in a cupboard somewhere, until the next clear out.

My uncles were steadily going through the garage boxes and had found a fair bit of stuff from my nan and grandad's house (their mum and dad) that they wanted to keep.

Uncle Ian even found his own amplifier and record deck! (Proper vintage now, and beautiful looking).

As Michael and Ian were both extremely good with their hands, being a brick layer and carpenter respectively, they also took power tools and some garden items.

At this point the skip was getting very full, so my uncle and son Tom jumped up and down to flatten it. It did help to create a bit more space, but we were having to be more precise in placement to capitalise on what space was left.

My aunts had found lots of cooking-related items and recipe books, including assorted cake tins and bowls. It made me think of how many hundreds, maybe even thousands, of cakes my mum had made using those items.

It was so sad to consider there would be no more from her, especially when she loved making and doing it so much.

When we cleared the freezer, there were cakes stored with Mum's handwriting on the label, but unfortunately they had been in there way too long to eat. I'm glad my aunts got rid of them on my behalf.

I feel sure there were probably quite a number of items it was probably better I didn't see. We did rather well on that first day and did make a good dent. Unbelievably, it had just been that. We agreed to reconvene the next day at 10am to allow everyone enough rest and recovery to start the process again.

I think we all slept rather well that night!

The next day came and with a sharp intake of breath we steeled ourselves to repeat the process. I had ordered another 10-yard skip in preparation for day two! Let's see how much of this one we can fill! It didn't take long.

The huge task of sorting was mixed with lots of cake, tea and good conversation. This really is where family and friends come together to make a difference. I was extremely grateful and told them as much.

The boxes in the roof were very nearly depleted, the garage was down to lower digit stacking, and today the shed was on the hitlist.

Dad had spent a fortune on monthly fees at a local storage company, and had decided to get a shed to store it all instead. It had made financial sense when the cost of the shed would be recouped over few of months, but did he need this stuff, really?

I had helped carry all the heavy stuff from storage and I

couldn't really understand at the time why Dad was keeping it, as I really couldn't see him using it. I was correct, one third went in the skip and the remainder to charity.

We found lots of flower arranging items, oasis/florist foam, sprayed dried flowers, posies, wiring, etc. It reminded me of the arrangements all over Spider Cottage and the previous homes before that. There had been none here because Mum wasn't able to use her hands by this point.

My mum had done all the flowers for our wedding. The standing arrangements throughout the church, arrangements on the pew ends, the marquee top table, the wedding cake and an individual arrangement for every table. A lot of work, but of course Mum loved to do it. It was another way to show her abundant love, which she was very generous with anyway.

We were all heads down working, when suddenly Lisa came rushing outside being very animated (even more than normal, and that's saying something!).

"I've found a will! I've found a will!!"

At last!

No wonder we hadn't found it before, as it was deep within a box that I'd just brought down from the loft!

What a relief!

Actually after this, and the difficulty in finding it, both Lisa and I got our own wills in order. It had been one thing we kept saying we'd get around to doing, but never did. As we would soon find out though, things on the will front were not that clear cut. There's a surprise! (Not!)

I haven't mentioned all the other trinkets we found yet!

Well, I can tell you there was a huge collection of bowls, cups, sauces, pots, dishes, etc., in many different shapes and designs, together with brass, silver and copper items, vases, glasses, statues, etc., etc., boxes and boxes and boxes!

The charity shop did very well from all of our items, but I know that some items had to be given elsewhere, as it was too good, even for our own charity shop!

We had made an even bigger dent today, but I think we all realised that it was too big a task to finish by close of day. So, it was agreed another weekend be chosen for round two, or maybe three and four! (Or ten!)

Whilst the relatives were here, they visited Mum at Holywell. They hadn't seen her in a little while, so they were quite shocked when they finally saw her. I know, because they told me. They, in fact, were very concerned as to whether Mum was getting the appropriate care needed, because of how she looked, I assured them she was.

I knew where they were coming from, but I suppose I had got used to seeing her gradual decline and had got used to it. I would imagine they were thinking the same as me. That, how is this even fair?

Mum weighed another couple of kgs less again now, despite the home giving her Complan meal replacements and trying to boost her food intake. She sometimes just didn't want to eat, but I always worried what would happen if that became a number of days in a row.

I thought of this more and more as Mum continued on her journey. I tried to comfort her, talk to her, be with her, but it was a one-way street. I had got used to her not interacting but I still tried and had even got used to the idea that she didn't know who I was.

I did try to believe that maybe, just maybe, there might be a tiny spark of recognition, but if there was I wasn't seeing it, despite my efforts.

I knew deep down that Mum loved me, she told me verbally and even wrote to tell me when we were apart, so there was no doubt.

I had wondered if she tried to make up for Dad, who despite being a man of many words, found it hard to express his feelings. It was no surprise when you understood his tough upbringing.

I missed that unconditional love.

It was only a few weekends after the first clearance that we were all back at it!

We pretty much used the same strategy as before - working in different areas of the house, so as to not get in each other's way. The lounge was still the central hub, with Lisa, Sue, and my aunts working away efficiently. Again, there was much laughter as more items were found and then discussed.

My mum's naughty sense of humour shone through here, as we found things like wind up willy toys, that jumped up and down across the floor. I can still hear her raucous laughter in my head now. My dad too had a good sense of humour, but it was probably a little more reserved in comparison.

We continued to find various items of interest and sorted accordingly, we also kept a pile of financial papers to shred or burn.

Two things we found today that I would definitely keep were the projector film slides and Dad's video cassette hand recorder, together with numerous tapes and videos.

Gold.

My dad loved to put on slide film shows, and whenever there was an opportune moment he would get his projector, put up a screen and we would delve into many nostalgic moments; Dad's travels in America including Yosemite and Disneyland, our house in Scotland, me growing up, French holidays, and lots of family members past and present, some of which were helping today!

The videos were labelled in his handwriting and included titles like, Josie Christmas 1999, France 2006, together with various family gatherings including Mum, Dad, Nan, Grandad, and all mum's cousins, and a spattering of various air shows thrown in for good measure.

I also found many, many photos that evoked a number of emotions, but now was not the time to sift through, I had to press on.

Today was fish and chips day. I felt we had all definitely earned it, so I took everyone's orders and went down to the local chippy. As always, it hit the spot! We all sat round, ate, drank and reminisced. Mum and Dad would have loved it.

The next day we started at 10.30am to allow for a short lie in. I think we were all feeling tired, not only physically but emotionally, not surprising really. Today I really felt like we made huge inroads.

The roof-space was now empty. The garage contained only stuff too good to throw away, together with Dad's workbench, fridge freezer and a chest freezer.

The big shed was all but empty and each box had been gone through and emptied, as much as possible.

In the lounge and conservatory, only the main big furniture was left; wicker chairs and settee, pine dining table and chairs, mahogany extendable table and chairs, a couple of display units and a drinks cabinet.

The drinks cabinet was an interesting one as it contained alcohol from many eras! All but very few bottles were kept, and the rest were put in the recycling.

Dubonnet, whisky, white and red wine, sherry, mulled wine, Southern Comfort, you name it, it was there!

We could have had one hell of a party, with a hell of an associated hangover too I think, especially with a cocktail of all those drinks!

I made the decision to keep some furniture in the house, to effectively stage it, when the time came to sell.

Dad and I had already cleared out the cupboards of Mum's clothes, and they had all gone to the charity shop. It felt very strange to get rid of all her clothes when she was still alive. For some reason it didn't feel right, but we knew she would never wear clothes like this again. I found that hard, as it felt very personal. I pictured her in certain items of clothing at various life events and felt a tinge of sadness. I think it's the finality of it all.

The fact that I would never see Dad in the flesh again too, and on reflection I recognised that I was grieving for 'Real Mum', as opposed to 'Alzheimer's Mum'.

I pictured her in my head, in her fancy ballgowns or even her winter coat and wellies going for a walk in the woods. Both of which I would never see again. She would continually live in nightgowns now.

Sad, because Mum loved her clothes, finding new items, and dressing up for special occasions.

With Dad's clothes too, it also made me think of where he had worn them. His black-tie suit which he wore to a dinner party on a submarine, the smart suits for the family get togethers and weddings, the string vest from his RAF days, and even the cravats he had worn for more casual get togethers. Each had a memory attached, and was also a stark reminder that he had gone.

Death is so final. I will never meet or chat face to face with Dad ever again. (Unless you believe in the afterlife - but who knows?!)

I'd like to believe there is something after death, and that you meet your loved ones, I really would, but I still reserve judgement, until I'm shown something more concrete. It's a lovely thought, and I want to believe it, but I'm still unsure.

We finished the day with a good old-fashioned cup of tea, and a natter in the conservatory. We had accomplished such a huge task. All rooms cleared, including the shed and garage. Only a few precious items in Dad's bedroom, and a few bits in the garage to keep.

We hugged and kissed each other goodbye, all agreeing that a huge task had been well accomplished, and that the house was much more Feng Shui aligned now.

CHAPTER FIFTEEN
BACK ON THE ROLLERCOASTER

After the satisfaction of breaking the back of the house, and feeling the love from those closest to us, our mood was always going to 'dip' when things returned to 'normal'.

The elation we felt at our achievement was always going to come back down to earth with a bump - seeing Mum again, and knowing I just had to support and love her the best I could.

She continued her mild but steady decline, making it very painful to observe. I'd noticed she was eating less and despite the home's efforts, it was an uphill battle to try and increase her weight to healthier levels.

She was now around the 26kg mark, which looking at it written down, is absolutely shocking. The staff at the home were doing their best, but I got the impression they felt her days were numbered. The thing is, we had been here before, many times.

I continued to go in, freshen the flowers, chat about my life, ensure the projection lights where on, and find some nice music to play.

I knew the music Mum loved, and played specific tracks, secretly hoping I might get a reaction, but this was sadly becoming less and less likely.

I can picture her now, singing along to her favourite tunes at Spider Cottage. We had always been similar in that way - enjoying music on in the background.

It was nearly her birthday, so she had some extra flowers in her room from our nearest and dearest, which made the whole room smell lovely. I was hoping it would bring up some great memories and feelings associated with her time surrounded by flowers as a florist. Funnily enough, it reminded *me* of going into the florists with her when I was younger, she was working extra hours and couldn't get someone to look after me. I enjoyed going in, it was always such fun.

At Mum and Dad's Golden Wedding Anniversary party, I was reminded, by her old boss Tony, that I had scratched my name into the outside of the cold room door. It was pretty obvious who was responsible!

I was famous for many years to follow.

Life carried on as normal (as normal as it could be) until that phone number came up on my phone again, the one that made me feel sick.

It was Holywell telling me Mum was not very well at all, and they thought I should go and see her. I got the impression things had escalated again, and I was extremely worried.

Lisa and I rushed to her side, and she was in bed looking gravely ill. She was struggling for breath, with her chest rising and falling much deeper than normal, as she tried to oxygenate her lungs. It was tough to watch.

Lisa and I looked at each other and without saying a word, we knew we both felt this time, it really might be it.

You think you are prepared but you aren't really. I thought, this really is it. The realisation was starting to sink in. It also struck me that the nurses seemed to be on high alert.

After a short while it was agreed to call the local GP to assess her condition. We waited for him as we sat with Mum, I held her hand and tried to comfort her, realising that it might be the last time.

The nurses ensured she had pain relief, but it was awful watching her struggle for breath.

The doctor came, assessed her, and confirmed our worst fears. He felt she had hours to live. I say worst fears because despite not wanting her to suffer anymore, I'd miss her terribly . She had been through such a lot, and I wanted her to be at peace. It had been a long, long, journey and it didn't need to be endured any more.

As you can imagine, the news from the doctor was like a sledgehammer. It surprised me actually, because I had been grieving for my mum for a long time now – first the real Mum and now the Alzeimer's Mum.

It was all so final and brought home to me that I would have now lost both parents, and in a relatively short space of time.

The doctor said, "Say what you need to say", but I had said it all before, many, many times.

Mum was given very strong drugs, on recollection, I think it was Morphine, to calm her and ease her pain. She was calmer, and despite what was happening, it did feel more serene and peaceful, as time wore on.

We stayed with her for hours and it was now getting quite late, (and past the few hours suggested by the doctor). She was sleeping, so one of the nurses said, "Look, if there's any changes we can call you, why don't you go home and try and get some sleep?"

We were initially reticent, but it was an enticing thought, and we *were* both shattered - emotionally battered and bruised.

Amazingly we did sleep, with one ear out and a phone nearby. When I woke, the first thing I did was ring the home, and they said, "Well, you won't believe this, but she appears to be ok now."

"What?!! What?!! Really?!"

"Yes, really!"

I went straight to Holywell to see her. She was conscious, and apart from looking tired, she displayed no overt signs of pain or discomfort, as she had the previous night. You could have knocked me down with a feather, and it was clear the morning staff coming in felt the same. 'Gobsmacked', as my mum would have said.

Some staff even did a double take, as they went past Mum's room.

One even said to me, "Well, I didn't expect to see her today!"

We were back on that rollercoaster again, but this time it was the extreme version with extra height and g-forces. Wow.

I made the most of being with Mum and held her hand trying to engage her.

She even had a drink and I fed her a little food.

One of the matrons brought me up a cup of tea and a few biscuits.

After this, I tried to get some of the legal wrangling sorted to ensure we didn't lose momentum when it came to the deputyship of Mum's care, and to look at the wills.

The solicitor assured me things were going in the right direction, but as these things do, it would take time.

One massive issue on finding the wills were that they were not the originals. We did not have the original signed ones, and we needed those.

The solicitor said I needed to find out where the wills were written. On the wills it said 'Co-Operative'. To cut a long story short, after proving who I was, the wills company said they would look for it, and after quite a while, it was found they only had digital copies and not the originals.

'Yep, that's about right isn't it?' I thought. Damn it.

It was suggested I try and track down the legal company who originally drew up the wills.

We searched high and low, through all the paperwork I'd kept at their house, for anything solicitor-related. I'd hoped they had use of a regular one for all legal matters, and after a long search we found a solitary solicitor's letter, asking if they would like to review their wills! Eureka!

I contacted her and explained the scenario and she said she would get back to me. It was a few days after, but true to her word she did. As you've probably guessed by now, it was not great news. No, she didn't have the original copy or any copy. Oh dear.

So where were the originals?

I contacted my solicitor and told her the news. It would complicate things and take longer, but we must proceed with what we had. Mum's deputyship had still not been completed, but we were getting closer.

Time marched on, and I decided to visit Ella, my middle daughter, who was studying at Brighton University.

I booked an AirBnB for a few days, so we could stay together in comfort.

It's a fair trek from our home, 3.5 hours on a good day, so I took my time. I had got as far as the M25 when I had a phone call from that dreaded number. Oh God. My heart skipped a beat.

I answered and it was Lois, one of the matrons at Holywell. She had quite a strong accent which was sometimes hard to understand but she said:

"Hello is that Stuart?"

I recognised her voice instantly, "Yes, it that Lois?"

"Yes Stuart, I'm sorry to have to tell you your mum has just passed away. She died this morning."

Pause.

I was trying to comprehend what has just been said to me.

Pause.

"Stuart, are you still there?"

I was there, I was just trying to absorb what was being said. She explained that Mum had been found in the morning and had peacefully passed away sometime during the night.

After the turbulence of the last few years, she had just peacefully slipped away, no fuss, no drama, she just left.

Luckily, there was a service station nearby, and I pulled over to take in the enormity of it all.

Mum had gone. She had finally got the peace she so desperately deserved. This. Was. In fact. It.

As the pent up emotion flooded my body, I burst into tears. They had been a long time coming.

I phoned Lisa straight away and told her. She was obviously upset and concerned, and we discussed our plan of action. I also decided there and then that I would ring Mum's two brothers and let them know. This was obviously upsetting, but I felt I had to do it. I needed to do it. I wanted to do it.

Lisa encouraged me to carry on my journey, but very carefully, as she was concerned about driving in the wake of such monumental news.

I deliberated, but did carry on to Brighton, as right at that moment I couldn't do much else. I was asked if I wanted to see Mum, but I really didn't.

I'd said many goodbyes, and she knew exactly how I

felt, so I didn't need closure by seeing her. Lisa did go up to see her and told me how peaceful she looked. Peace, at last. It did help to know that.

In some weird way, as much as I was hugely upset at her passing, I think there was an element of relief. She did not have to put up with Alzheimer's anymore, and my God, it had taken a toll. My poor mum who wouldn't hurt a fly, endured such an awful thing for such a long time.

We will never know how cognisant she was of the progression of her disease, but I had always hoped she hadn't felt too frightened or confused. She did know we were there for her all the way, and I hoped we did it the way she would have wanted.

It's an extremely hard conversation to have. As we didn't have the benefit of hindsight, we didn't know her exact wishes before she became too ill to tell us, we had to guess.

If you are facing this situation, I would strongly urge you to discuss and document your loved one's wishes, before it's too late. We didn't, and I really wish we had. You believe you are doing your best, but it's much better to know you are fulfilling someone's wishes, exactly as they wanted. Consider aspects such as chosen care homes, power of attorney, specific funeral wishes, specific end of life care, and any personal aspects required by them. It's tough doing this prior to illness or event but can save future heart ache.

I carried on driving to my AirBnB steadily. Normally there would have been music blaring as I drove, but this time I travelled in silence. I stayed focused, but needed to process what I'd just been told.

I parked up, found the flat, got the keys from the key box and entered.

What a wonderful flat! Immaculately furnished with an open plan raised kitchen and dining room, and lower level lounge. On the table were some chocolates and some wine - how kind. I dropped my clothes in one of the bedrooms and sank into the sofa.

I did turn on the TV, but it was just background noise. I texted Ella to say I had arrived and confirmed the address. I was pleased just to sit down and relax, something I very rarely did these days.

I had already spoken to Lisa and she knew we wanted to use the same funeral director's that had dealt with both our dads' funerals. She let the home know, and they arranged for Mum to be collected.

I feel sure they would have been surprised at the frequency that we were using their services. To quote an exclamation my Mum used quite a lot – 'garden peas and custard!'

If ever there was an upmarket middle class swear word, I think that wins the prize!

I'm still not really sure where it came from, but it's very endearing.

In a way it was good to be totally away from home with Ella. We decided to order dinner through Deliveroo, as I didn't fancy going out, understandably.

Luckily after eating, I felt sleepy. The bed was really comfy and I got off to sleep quickly. I was shattered.

When I woke up in the morning, my first thoughts were of Mum and the reality started to sink in.

Ella showed me around Brighton and it was good to get out in the fresh air. We visited The Lanes and some of the various quirky independent shops Brighton is known for.

I can see why Ella had chosen Brighton for her University studies; it was edgy, vibrant, and there was lots going on.

Soon enough, it was time to leave and I hugged Ella tightly as we said our goodbyes. The journey back was uneventful, which in itself is always good thing, especially when you are driving for a number of hours.

When I got home, Lisa gave me a huge hug (always very much appreciated) and we sat and chatted through events of the last few days.

There was so much to organise. So, I set to and compiled a list. Dad's funeral having been so recent made things easier because I already had all the contacts I needed and knew what I was doing. (Well, more than the first time.)

I made a point of going up to Holywell the following day because it was important to settle all outstanding bills, clear Mum's room and thank the staff for all their dedication, love and support. This was not something I was looking forward to obviously, as it would be the first time I would set foot inside without Mum being there.

I parked outside and waited a few moments, composing myself. I knew this was going to be tough.

I went in and saw several of the key staff members and it was all very emotional, as you can imagine. This felt just like going back to Dad's empty house after he died. The room was soulless, but seeing Mum's personal belongings brought it all home - she was gone forever.

Her hairbrush which I used to brush her hair, still had her hair in it.

She so loved having her hair brushed.

When she was able to show emotion, you could tell she really enjoyed it, as much as I enjoyed doing it for her. I can picture her blissful face now.

She was the same when I gave her facials (probably executed very poorly compared to the professionals) but she still enjoyed it despite my amateur touch.

Her soft toys - Bagpuss and Tatty Teddy, her nightgowns, her Christmas lights and even the big photo frame I'd left in her room, so the staff could get an idea of what she *was* like, before the Alzheimer's.

I looked at those photos and thought about those happier times - Mum and I in Scotland with me in fancy dress, Dad sat with Mum having a great time on a trip to York, a black and white shot of Mum with beehive hair from the 60s, and one of her in a long purple crushed velvet ball gown looking very glamorous.

How could anyone guess these photos would become a snapshot of happier times, or how life would turn out years later?

Is it better not to know? Perhaps.

I decided to gift Holywell a lot of Mum's items; her TV, her expensive wheelchair, her nightgowns, etc, as I knew they would be gratefully received and useful to them.

I went into the office, settled the bill and saw the lovely ladies I always chatted to in there.

They wanted to give me back Mum's petty cash, and I said, "Put it in your Christmas pot."

I did actually go back at Christmas to deliver two big boxes of selection packs, so that all the staff got something as a small token of my appreciation.

So Holywell was all done and dusted. It felt strange to know I would no longer be visiting as I had done so often over the years. I believe she had been going there for over 4 years, whether it was a just for the day or after, as a resident.

It still feels weird when I occasionally drive past not to call in.

So, to the funeral planning.

I got the wheels in motion as before, speaking to the funeral director to organise the details. I decided, better the devil you know, (I'm not too sure that's an apt saying, in these circumstances, but it's true), that I'd stick with the formula I had already used.

I contacted Marion, the pastor, who was shocked and dismayed to hear I would need her services again so soon. We worked out the best date for the service, booked the crematorium, started designing the service, thought about appropriate music, and spoke to the florist. (Who was equally shocked, that I was organising another funeral so close to the last one).

As Mum had been a florist, I wanted to ensure the flowers were a true representation of her abilities and the work she so enjoyed. I spoke in depth to the florist, explained Mum's history and we worked together to pick the best options and colours. I wanted the flowers on her casket to make a real statement, and we also talked about having a huge stand arrangement that spread out and down. I also got her to do a 'MUM' in flowers and ribbons, just like my own mum had done.

The stand arrangement was not for the service, this was for our house. Lisa and I agreed to have a tea at ours for the wake. This would be just like she used to do with sandwiches, cakes, biscuits etc., and of course, plenty of tea.

We dug out all the old china cups and saucers and even sourced doilies. I know she would have approved.

I had to get the order of service written, so the funeral director could print it. Again, it was so important that it represented Mum and her life appropriately.

I had already seen, as a sample, a beautiful service programme that had flowers as borders and knew that I wanted to have that.

We chose the hymn, 'Morning has Broken' and I chose some songs to play when she came in to the crematorium, for contemplation, reflection, and when she was leaving.

Choosing the music really set me off, as it had before. As I said, I absolutely love my music and I really *feel* it. Mum felt it too.

I once read that when engrossed in a good book, for

those that really get into it, you are right in-between the pages, right within the letters and words. It was the same for me with music, being within its framework and within the notes and words.

Every detail had to be perfect.

Mum had devoted so much of her life to me, and I was hugely grateful. I wanted everyone who came to the funeral to not only *know* that, but *feel* it too.

The entry music I chose was - Me and Mrs Jones by Billy Paul. I can see her singing along to this, she loved romantic soul songs, and she particularly loved this one.

The two reflecting songs were Always and Forever by Heatwave, another slow, soul ballad, and of course had to include a Christmas song. (Even though it was November, because as I'd said, she used to play them way before Christmas). There were so many she knew, enjoyed singing and loved to listen to, but the one that really stood out was 'The Christmas Song' by Nat King Cole. Perfect.

The exit music was Reunited by Peaches and Herb, another soul ballad, so fitting for many reasons.

Nobody had come forward to say they would do a reading or to speak about Mum, so I felt, no matter how hard, I *had* to speak. I was determined. This time, I *had* to do it. As I said before, I hadn't spoken at Dad's funeral and despite writing out what I wanted to say and Marion reading it, I regretted not doing it myself.

I was getting butterflies thinking about it, because of the enormity of the task, but I was absolutely certain I had to at least try. I had spoken about it to Marion, the pastor, and she said, if it all got too emotional, she would step in.

I put together some photographs of Mum and chose ones to include in the order of service. I chose ones that I felt represented her and her personality the best, and I included one with me, and one with my Dad too.

The service schedule was sent, double checked and proof read. It looked great, even if I did say so myself.

Everything was coming together, and I was looking forward to closing this chapter of our lives. Whether I would experience 'closure', only time would tell.

I had taken two weeks off work again, to focus on getting everything organised, and I needed it. Luckily clients understood.

The day of the funeral arrived, and I woke with those familiar butterflies in my stomach again.

All my kids were busily getting their very smart funeral attire together, and I was watching the clock to ensure everything was on time.

I *hate* being late. With a passion. I'd rather be an hour early than five minutes late, although I'm not too sure that would serve so well today.

I can remember going to my nan Phyllis's funeral, and embarrassing myself by waving at a few people waiting as I arrived, only to realise it was people from the funeral before. Then as soon as we finished, there were people milling around directly outside, waiting for the next one. It had felt so impersonal and rushed.

The house was already up together, all neat and tidy, as everyone was coming back to ours afterwards. This had turned out to be a huge task, but it is what Mum would have wanted, and so worth all the effort. I even bought a hot water urn, so we didn't have to keep boiling the kettle every five minutes.

I saw the cars for the funeral procession arrive outside and Mum's casket surrounded by all the beautiful flowers.

It looked stunning, just as I'd hoped. The butterflies were now doing 'loop the loops'.

I chivvied my lot along and we all got in the main car, as I sat contemplating what was to come this morning. I don't often, but I prayed silently that I had the strength to get through the day.

As the car and Mum's casket drew up to the crematorium, I could already see many familiar faces. I was trying to hold it all together and stay as calm as I could.

Once again me, my son Tom, my Uncle Ian and one of

the funeral staff would carry Mum's coffin.

The familiar, 'Me and Mrs Jones' music came out of the speakers, and at that point we knew it had started. We carried Mum in and rested her in front of the congregation. The weight of the coffin was stark in contrast to my dad's, no weight at all.

Marion welcomed everyone in her calming manner, we sung 'Morning has Broken', and then it was my turn to speak. Even though my emotions were extremely raw, I drew on an inner strength to complete one of the last tasks I could do for Mum.

I went up to the lectern, looked out at the sea of faces, and took a big breath.

Here's what I said:

My Mum

I've always believed in Karma; that is until my Mum contracted Alzheimer's. The disease that ripped out the very core of her being.

I still don't know what she did to deserve this affliction. She was selfless and harmed no one.

She taught me to put others first, and always led by this example.

The gregarious, natural, 'people-person' disappeared into a hollow shell.

Over the years, as the disease took hold, there were occasional glimpses of the 'old Di', but these were fleeting, and what was left was a mere shadow of her former self.

The Mum who had wiped away my tears, and listened to my woes, had well and truly disappeared, quite some time ago.

In truth, I've been grieving for my real mum for many years now, but it still came as a shock when she passed.

It's important to remember all the good times we all enjoyed with her, because whilst Alzheimer's was part of her life journey, it didn't define her.

The expert cook and cake maker, the amazingly talented florist, the proud homemaker. The loving aunt, grandmother, friend, daughter, sister, and mother.

Mum loved people, and this was so evident in social situations, where her buoyant laugh could be heard echoing, amongst all the other guests.

She loved a good party, and this was never more evident than at our wedding. She *so* looked forward to that day and was in her element. Socialising, dancing, chatting, and beaming ear to ear, on what was probably the hottest day of the year.

A perfect example of this was when most of the guests

were joined in a big circle on the dance floor, passing their hand through their legs to the next person, doing the elephant dance!

Mum was laughing and beaming as usual.

I will never forget the receiving line on our wedding day where in typical Mum's effusive fashion, she tightly hugged Lisa's Dad, Bo!

Bo, not really used to much 'hugginess' was a little unsure of what to do when this effervescent woman grabbed him so tightly!

Looking even further back I remember when I had Chicken Pox at the age of 17 (which meant it was a more virulent strain), Mum, not only running me cool baths and dabbing me with Calamine Lotion, but playing Scrabble with me to take my mind off of the scratching- all at 3am!

I've received some lovely messages of support since my Mum's passing, together with several reminders of lovely memories.

All of these tell of a beautiful soul, who would do anything for anybody.

Welcoming arms open to whoever needed them, and any chance to prepare food for whoever needed it. Food prepared with passion and love, in the blink of an eye, as only Di could do!

So many wonderful family occasions catered by her -

Christmases, Easters, my 16th, 18th and 21st birthday parties. In fact, there really didn't need to be a reason, for her to happily feed anyone!

In this day and age, where mental health awareness is so front of mind, Mum would give a listening ear to anybody who needed it, it didn't matter who they were.

As a true, gentle, genuine giving person, she would have offered the shirt off her back to anybody in need. She was just happy to give, in any way needed.

I remember the local council digging up the road outside Mum and Dad's house.

She was so pleased they were sorting it, she came out with homemade sandwiches, cakes and biscuits, and a pot of tea served in bone china tea cups, with doilies no less!!

(Yes, mum loved her paper doilies!!)

I still feel sure, to this day, there's an urban myth going around of a lovely lady in Lower Stanton St Quinton, who gave these workman a high tea and food fit for a king!!

In closing, I must also mention my mum's love of Christmas, something that seems to have been inherited by our beautiful daughter Liv.

It appears Christmas isn't just for December! As Liv and my mum would start playing Christmas tunes and watching Christmas films, many months before!

(As early as August in some cases!)

I give my deep, heartfelt thanks to all the staff at Holywell Nursing Home and the amazing matron, nurses and carers, who provided the best possible care for my mum.

They made her last few years more comfortable, manageable, and bearable, something for which I will be eternally grateful.

I just wish they had all known the pre Alzheimer's Mum that *we* all knew and loved, but hopefully these tales today, give an insight into her character.

She gave me something so, so precious.

Not only wonderful memories, but that true, rare commodity: unconditional, love.

I will remember her and her love forever.

I hope she realises how much I loved her, and just how grateful I am for all the time we spent together, and what she did for me.

Of course, as my mum's son, I feel extremely honoured and proud to have grown up and be nurtured by such a kind soul, with a big heart.

Here's to you Mum. I love you.

I sat down, relieved I had completed my first major task for today, one more to go. Always and forever comes over the speakers, time for reflection. Lisa held my hand.

Marion, the pastor, said a few words and then Nat King Cole's famous recording 'The Christmas Song' came on. That did get me a bit. I thought of all the lovely family Christmases we had enjoyed together - the decorations, the food, the good times. It was Mum's favourite time of the year.

To honour Mum, I also wrote and read a poem of what I thought she would want to say now, having been through what she had.

It went like this;

WHAT DIANA WOULD LIKE TO SAY TODAY

Prior to my Alzheimer's I had a good life,
Not too much to call trouble or strife,
Of course, I wanted to do much more with my life,
But it wasn't meant to be.

Please don't cry or be upset for me,
Remember the good times and all the love with my family,
I still have those previous memories of times past,
Although it was tough holding onto those to the last.

I still remembered my mum, dad, and two lovely brothers,

The ladies, 41 club, Baldwins and others,

When you reflect back at life you realise it's the people
that mean so much more ,

Not the material things, coveted by many.

I always tried to live life to my best,

Which hopefully is evident in the photos nearest,

The dinner parties, the get togethers and all the family
gatherings,

Just thinking of all the cakes made and candles blown
out,

That always had my blessings.

Think of me in Heaven now and finally at peace,

No battle to fight, no pain, what a release.

I can finally be with the love of my life, dear Colin my
love, together forever, your dear wife.

So, as I close my thoughts go to you,

Dear listeners, my loved ones and the family I knew.

Make sure you make each day count, for you never
know what's around the corner and the hills you must
surmount.

Be happy, be free, believe you can do it, and I will be up

here, looking over you, cheering with good spirit.

I had done it. A bit wobbly in a couple of parts, but I did it. Relief.

Marion led The Lord's Prayer, said her closing words and then we gathered around Mum's casket while her leaving song played – 'Reunited'. She was going to be with Dad in their final resting place. Together forever.

Close family only gathered around the graveside, and we listened to Marion's lovely calming words, threw dirt, lay flowers, and said our final goodbyes.

Rest in peace Mum, finally.

Mum had dealt with Alzheimer's for over 7 years with the more serious issues raising their heads around the age of 65. I've been trying to work out the timeframes, as there was a grey area prior to diagnosis, but I think she was diagnosed around five years prior to her death, she had just had her 72nd birthday.

That's an awfully long time to be slowly declining. Seven very painful years.

Despite my love for Mum, I was pleased she did not have to endure this torture any longer. It had been just over one year since Dad had died, and an awful lot had happened within that year. I think we had the annual pass to the most extreme of rollercoasters, but at last the ride was stopping and we were able to step off.

After the funeral, we went back to our house and enjoyed a feast fit for a king (or queen), together with lots of tea.

Surprisingly, I was already starting to feel the 'release'. I had some lovely comments on the funeral, some saying it was the best one they had been to, and people felt it had been very fitting, which was exactly what I'd hoped for.

The guests stayed for a couple of hours or so. I think they understood it had been a very emotional day, and we would all be tired. They were right.

CHAPTER SIXTEEN
SELLING THE HOUSE

After Mum's funeral there were still quite a few house things to sort out, legal estate work to be done, preparing the house to sell, and organising the headstone for the grave.

With Mum's passing the need for the Deputyship of the Court of Protection also passed, so I contacted the solicitor to let her know. She was saddened by the news and I asked for the bill for the completed work to be forwarded as soon as possible - I wanted that particular chapter of this story closed.

Along with preparing the house, the garden needed a tidy up and I found a gardener to just 'blitz' it. The prompt came from a neighbour, who rung me to ask when was I going to sort my garden out! Little did he know what we'd been through just to get to this stage.

The gardener did a great job mowing the grass back to

reasonable levels, trimming and weeding where possible, and just generally tidying. After that, it was much easier for me to keep on top of it.

Even though I knew it would be a lot of work to get the house on the market, I was determined to keep the momentum going.

We had done so well in clearing and sorting, and to be honest, I suppose with both Mum and Dad gone, it was another task towards gaining more closure.

Whilst I didn't particularly enjoy going back to the house, I think as it now contained fewer personal items it was a little easier. Plus, I hadn't grown up in this house, or even lived there.

I decided to stage the house for sale. This meant I had purposely left certain key items to make it looked lived in, albeit a little sparse.

There are two schools of thought when it comes to 'staging'. Some believe it is to show a house when it is completely empty, to make it easier for the buyers to see themselves in it, while others believe it should appear lived in, so prospective buyers can get a sense of how it looks with furniture.

I prefer the second theory.

I left some pictures on walls, the TV, one bed, sofas, chairs, sideboards, conservatory furniture, the dining room table and a few of Mum's knick-knacks on window ledges, etc.

After our mammoth clear out, there were still two areas that needed work; Dad's old bedroom, and the garage. If you remember, his old bedroom had been used to store items we needed to keep (including papers to sort through), and the garage which still contained some stuff we considered 'useful'.

I spent nearly a whole day going through the bedroom, and found some amazing photographs and slides. They spanned many years, from black and white ones of Dad and Mum when they were 'courting', to a holiday in Scotland, way before we moved up there. Some childhood photos of me from baby to teenager, and even some I'd taken from my school days. A few from a Norfolk Broads school trip, brought back two very distinct memories. One was of my friend Gary and I doing something we were told expressly not to do, i.e. jumping in the water! Our punishment was to clean the toilets for the rest of the holiday!

The other memory was of us trying to conceal alcohol aboard the boat, being discovered by the teachers and them making us watch as they enjoyed every last drop! (Served us right).

I found lots of Dad's work-related stuff that needed to

be burnt or shredded. When we were allowed (post COVID-19), one of my clients, who has a woodland and owns an incinerator, very kindly offered to help deal with it.

The slides again covered many years and by putting them up to the window light, I was treated to a snapshot through many different countries and decades of both mine, and my parents' lives.

Quite a few featured French trips with the Round Table and Ladies Circle trips with friends, and our trips to France as a family. Also slides from our regular get togethers with my nan, grandad, uncles, aunts, and many cousins; at Christmas, Easter and Bonfire night. I loved them all, but especially the latter as we all brought fireworks, my grandad built a huge bonfire, and my nan made the table groan with a huge feast of food!

I went through a huge box of photos and threw away any of people I didn't recognise, and kept the rest. My dad was probably the most prolific recorder of both video film and photographic material in our entire family. He kept that up throughout his life, and I'm certainly glad he did, as it was a lovely record and something to treasure.

The garage still contained a fair few items I thought were either too good for charity or had some use for us, but eventually we arranged for a clearance company to take it away. We had enough stuff anyway!

When I was looking around the house, I noticed in parts it needed decorating, especially Mum's bedroom and the hallway. This was partly due to her wheelchair banging into doorframes and walls, but also I wanted to brighten up the entrance, with a fresh brilliant white coat of paint. First impressions and all that.

At this time, due to COVID-19, I had to close my business for a period of time.

National guidelines, together with local authority guidance forced us to shut, while more people were vaccinated and to allow the numbers of contagious people to drop.

This was obviously disastrous for my business, but it also gave me way more time to tackle things such as decorating, 'making good', and tidying. We even ordered skips for our own house and did a clearance there too. In fact, just this week, we decided to get another skip. When the driver came back to pick it up, he commented that we couldn't have anything left in the house!

I set to work painting Mum's bedroom. Dad had changed a doorway to allow better access into that room for both the carers and the wheelchair, and the plaster was still only partially painted. Mum's hoist was still in place, and I considered removing it, but it was still attached to the roof electrics, so I decided to leave it.

Mum's hospital bed had already gone, and as Dad's bed had seen better days I got rid of that too, making it much easier to get around the room.

It was already looking so much better.

I had learnt over the years to remove fixtures and fittings where possible before beginning, and to also use Frog Tape to mask off areas not to be touched. It improved the quality of my work substantially, but there again, it was at a low base to start with!

I made sure to apply two coats of paint, so it covered well and didn't appear patchy. One tricky aspect was above the entrance to Mum's bedroom. There was effectively two wooden 'flaps' to allow the hoist to operate. Again, as I'm not known for my DIY prowess, I left it as was and just painted that too!

As is usual, the fresh white paint made the skirtings look off white, so I glossed those over. Dad had laid new wooden laminate flooring throughout the bedrooms and hallways. In fact, I had suggested it, and got a guy to quote, as it made clearing up the 'messes' a lot easier.

Once the bedroom was finished, I planned to do the entrance hall too, so the standard of décor blended together better. I did both hallways, ceilings and up the stairs. Quite a bit more work, but I knew it would look so much better, plus I had the luxury of time on my hands.

After a number of days, I had completed it all and it looked so much better. It gave a nice first impression as you stepped in, so I was very happy. The rest of the paintwork in the house was fine, so I left that as it was. I paid for a cleaner to deep clean the whole house top to bottom, and it looked a lot better for it.

I also paid for a carpet cleaner to come in and go through the lounge, as around where Dad had sat there were a few food stains and marks, and there were soot stains near the fire hearth. Once they had done it all, it looked great once again!

I made sure the garden was well presented, and I felt like the house was ready to sell - quite an achievement, everything considered.

I had already noted a few estate agents, and organised three to come round and give us a valuation. I decided that was enough to get a good range.

House prices had gone up a little during the four years my parents had been at the house, so I was intrigued to hear their thoughts on the house, and what their valuation would be.

I met each agent, and they valued the house within about a £30k variance. I felt the first estate agent wanted to pitch it low and sell quick, and the other two valued it pretty similarly. I decided to think on what to do. I was not in any particular rush, but at the same time it would be nice not to have to worry about it anymore.

After much deliberation I decided to go with C.J. Hole. It was a father and son team, who had actually sold this very house to my parents when they bought it. They seemed very professional, looked presentable, and I had to trust my gut instinct once again - it's generally quite a good judge!

They took photographs and wrote the blurb, I proof read it and signed it off. The house was finally for sale! Yay!

There were a number of viewings within the first few weeks and a smattering after, then things slowed. We had feedback that the house was nice and well presented, but nobody wanted to put in an offer yet.

I waited a little longer before speaking to the estate agent. We decided to lower the price and see what happened. There was an instant market reaction to this, and quite a number of viewers came to take a look.

After this, we did get an offer which I accepted, after some negotiation. They would be in a chain, but nothing too big.

I needed to fill in some paperwork and answer lots of questions relating to the property, which was really difficult having never owned it myself or having access to all the original paperwork that went with it. Things like whether the conservatory was BS compliant, or whether a flood survey was completed, or who the solar panels where installed by, and who the feed in tariff was with. This enabled Dad to effectively sell the surplus electricity generated, back to the grid. Even simple enquiries about electricity suppliers were difficult to answer, as Dad had kept switching.

I won't bore you with the number of calls, how long spent on hold, and how many times I was invited to choose option one, two, or three! But I now have a bald patch, which I swear was from me pulling my hair out, trying to get the answers I needed!

Things progressed, and the prospective owners organised a survey.

The survey was completed, and from what we understood nothing of importance was flagged up, however later that week after the prospective owners went to measure up for curtains, etc. they messaged the estate agents and said that they wanted to pull out of the sale!

What?!

It turned out they had heard about a green-light building development in the field next to the house, and were concerned about the impact, as there was planning for six new dwellings.

There was a little oblong of grazing pasture right to the back of the house, but this was the field next to that. There had been planning on it for a while because of a dilapidated shed, and now planning had been finally granted.

This had been put on the property particulars, as far as I knew, but obviously it was a bigger issue than we first thought.

I spoke to C.J. Hole, and we agreed to put the house back on the market at the same lower price at which we had received the offer. I then spoke to my solicitor too, to ensure nothing further needed to be done on the existing house contract, to be ready for the next potential sale.

There was a fair bit of interest when it went back on the market, interestingly from people that had liked the look of it before, but then realised they had been too late when the previous offer came in.

After a few weeks, and the initial disappointment, we had two offers on the same day, both expressing how much they had liked it, and one lady saying she had struggled to sleep thinking about it!

We received an offer for the full asking price from one buyer and another for £5k more than the asking price! I did accept the higher offer, as she had been so keen on the house.

Funnily enough, I went back around the house with Lisa to turn the heating back down after the viewings, and a chap who had been working on the house next door approached us. He asked whether we were the owners and I said yes.

He then went to explain how he had made the offer on our house that had been turned down. He said that the house would have been perfect for looking after his elderly dad, and wondered why I had turned down his full asking price. I explained why, and I did feel terrible for him, but I hoped he understood.

Later that day, he put in another offer matching that of the other buyer, but as we had already accepted another offer, we felt it would be unfair to pull out. I felt for him, but I also couldn't let the lady down who had been so keen. My dad had been gazumped a number of times and I certainly wasn't going to do it to anyone else.

Luckily, I had already filled in what questions I could on the house paperwork from our previous 'false-start' and some of that information could be reapplied to this sale.

The prospective owner had searched and found me through social media, and used messenger to message me direct. I was a little unsure at first, as I thought communication should have been kept through the estate agents and solicitors, but nevertheless, I answered.

As COVID-19 had taken hold quite badly, C.J. Hole's policy of viewings was 20 minutes maximum, so she asked me if she could do a longer viewing with me, and if I was willing to open up and leave them to it.

I decided to agree to their suggestion, only if I kept the estate agents in the loop. They were happy for that to happen, and a date and time was set.

I opened up, the heating back on and waited outside. They arrived, we exchanged pleasantries, and it was agreed they would contact me when they were done. I was a little surprised at how long they were taking, but just over two hours later, they rang and said they had checked everything.

They asked me further questions, which I answered to the best of my knowledge, bearing in mind I had never lived in the house, or dealt with the initial legal documents.

They had thoroughly checked heating, appliances, lighting, garage, roof space, etc. and had a number of 'snagging' points and requests, which they requested we remedy, before we signed the contract.

I must admit, initially I thought it was a little cheeky, but then I thought in the whole scheme of things, and considering the overall house sale price, it was a small ask in comparison. I also, luckily, had time to sort these things as I was not working, so I went ahead and started tackling the list.

I had to contact professionals for some things, like electrical testing, light replacement, gas and heating checks, fire replacement and getting rid of the hoist. I actioned these immediately, but these tradesmen were very busy, so it took a few weeks to do. Again, in the scheme of things, it hadn't taken that long really to tick and score my list! Phew!

I also had to organise the solar panel feed in tariff reading. It had been a real headache, as the company that installed the panels had gone into receivership and we didn't have any of the associated paperwork. The solicitor helped track down the feed in tariff company, and I was surprised to eventually find out that, despite it all being operational, Dad had never registered!

All those years, and he hadn't earned any money from having it!

The house sale was going through nicely, together with all the associated paperwork, I was so looking forward to seeing the back end of that!

As a previous NVQ assessor and verifier I was used to paperwork, but it definitely was not my forté.

We set the date to exchange contracts for the beginning

of April, and finally we had a date to aim towards. I felt like it was going to happen, after all this effort.

Now I knew the house sale was well on the way, there was the task of emptying the house of all the items I'd used to stage it.

I decided to take pictures and measurements and make up descriptions of everything and list them on Facebook Marketplace.

Over the next few weeks, after many messages, texts and calls, and meeting lots of lovely people, I had managed to get rid of it all! Hoorah!

I helped an older lady's two sons take the mahogany dining room table and chairs on their garden clearance van. I helped a lovely old chap with the sofa and chairs on multiple trips, who would have it as a stop gap before getting his new one. There was another guy who was up-cycling the pine set of conservatory table and chairs, and so on, and so on.

It was great to meet all these people and know that Mum and Dad's furniture would go on to live another life. It all went for peanuts, but it was an awful lot better than going to land fill.

The house sale went through and I must say it was with a huge sigh of relief, because it had been such a huge collective effort.

I reiterated just how grateful I was to all those involved in it and organised a meal and a get together as a small token of my appreciation.

I don't know if you believe in these things, but as I locked up the house for the very last time before leaving the keys for the new owners, I closed the door, and watched a robin on the fence post right by me, just sit and look around.

It sat there looking for quite some while, and I just stood there and observed it. They are my favourite birds, so beautiful.

Now if you believe in the theory, robins are supposed to signify hope, renewal, a rebirth, and a sign of good things to come. It also can mean that loved ones are near.

Now, I had never seen a robin in their garden, so to me it seems a bit more than just a coincidence. I did feel something, but I can't really tell you what. I really did feel it was a sign from my lovely mum and dad, they did feel close.

I took some solace from it. I told Lisa as soon as I got home, and even shared it on my social media. Lisa felt it was indeed a sign from above, a notion which was certainly supported from other friends on Instagram and Facebook.

In the background of the house sale, I was making efforts on Mum and Dad's headstone. I had already looked around the graveyard for some inspiration as they all varied so much. There was currently a wooden cross and plaque marking the spot, but it was time to organise something more permanent.

I had already done my own survey in my head, taking in the stone types, shapes, and letter fonts. It had reminded me of a school graveyard survey I had done, many years ago, where we had to look for the earliest headstones. I found the 'Christmas' family, and to my amusement I found a Mary Christmas! (It was probably funnier at the time).

I had found a dark stone I liked, chosen the lettering font and colour, and had chosen a shape I liked. I had also decided to include a photograph of Mum and Dad kissing, as it felt right.

Here are the words I chose:

TOGETHER. FOREVER

Two beautiful souls.
Who showed us all how love should be.
Greatly missed, loved and appreciated.
Now finally at peace.

When the headstone was erected I arranged a get together, so close family members could see it. As soon as I saw it in its place, I was confident it looked right, and that it was fitting. Thank goodness.

Lisa's mum, Sue, visits Bo's grave every week, and tends to my mum and dad's at the same time. They are only two graves away from each other. We really do appreciate it. I visit on special occasions now mostly, but do pop up when the mood takes me.

I always play my music and speak to them.

CHAPTER SEVENTEEN
THE FINAL HURDLE

With the house sorted and the bills paid, there was a big, satisfying tick on my to do list.

I thought back to the initial list(s) which had been so long, it was so nice to see just one shorter list left.

I had been in touch with my solicitor to tidy loose ends and settle any outstanding matters. It had been a huge, long and complicated journey, I couldn't have done it without her, and I was extremely grateful.

The COVID-19 pandemic had complicated matters further, with staff on furlough, some working from home, and most offices just manned by a skeleton staff. This made an already complicated scenario that much harder. I think because of all the aforementioned issues, it took the best part of two years to sort all the legal paperwork from start to finish. It's hard to put a time frame on sorting and finding paperwork but it was many, many hours.

I haven't discussed this before, as I think money is always such a contentious issue, and it had never been a focus for me. I had been motivated in life to continually improve, and to be a better person, but money was never a key driver. I wanted to do well at my job, and make an impact, and I can honestly say I took pride in everything I did.

I always worked hard, something instilled in me by my parents. My dad wanted to better himself and rose up the ranks in various jobs, and in his spare time, he was always doing DIY or tinkering on a car, etc.

Mum worked hard to supplement our income, and at one point paid for my private education. She worked way before it seems most mothers had to, like it is nowadays.

The money to me was not a motivator, but at the same time I wanted to ensure my kids had a healthy and prosperous life, that we weren't on the breadline and we had a good standard of living.

I had worked very long hours, for many years as a personal trainer, as most of my work was either before most people's days began or at the end of the standard working day, although I did have some day clients too. I got up at 5 am, left at 6 and opened up the gym at 6.45 ready to start at 7am. I then generally worked until 8 or 8.30pm, back at 9 or 9.30 pm, and I worked a Saturday morning. Then I was off from early Saturday afternoon until late Monday afternoon. So I felt that I had accrued many hours of work along the way and had 'earnt' my early retirement.

I look back fondly back on those times. It always makes me smile when I remember how Lisa and I would swap over childcare duties, when I would finish work and Lisa would start. I usually had to warn my last appointment that we might be 'descended' upon. Five minutes before the final session finished the kids, in turn, would look through the letterbox all excited, and then as soon as that door opened, they came in like Tasmanian devils, running around and exercising on the equipment as if their lives depended on it!

I guess what money can do, is give you choice and options, and the inheritance from Mum and Dad gave us just that. I was trying to think of the best way of investing their hard-earned money, whilst being fair to my family, and in a way Mum and Dad would have approved of.

I spoke to my family about an idea I felt would be fair to everyone. I suggested we invest the money in property, but not just any property, a holiday home in our favourite place - Ibiza.

Everyone agreed to this, especially Ella and Josie, who had already been clubbing out there with their friends. In their eyes it was a free holiday - just sort the flights!

Previously, this was just a pipe dream. In fact, it wasn't even that. I had never thought I'd be in a position to own a dustbin in Ibiza, let alone a property.

We started looking excitedly, and had already been watching the TV programme, 'A Place in the Sun', for inspiration. We had checked through the Spanish Idealista app, which contained many properties on the market in Ibiza.

One thing I quickly realised though was that Ibiza, or Eivissa as it's known, is the most expensive area of all the Balearics or Spain to buy a property. I was always amazed on the programme at the detached properties bought in southern Spain for £125,000 for example, but in Ibiza you'd be lucky to even find a one bed flat for that price.

One thing in the back of my mind was that I had heard horror stories of ex-pats buying properties abroad without exactly the right planning consents or legal paperwork (through no fault of their own), and then losing the property and their money.

My dad's sister Margaret and her husband lost their property in Spain due to some dodgy builder dealings and after all this effort, I certainly didn't want that happening to us.

I did some research into getting official help in Spain -

someone trustworthy who could help us navigate the system. There is an excellent Facebook group called 'Ibiza Winter Residents', which is populated mainly by people living on the island full time, as well as those with holiday homes.

I created a post and sent out to all in the group, explaining that we were in an unexpected position to buy a property, due to my mum and dad's very sad demise. I asked if anyone could recommend someone to help us with our purchase based on personal experience.

I had loads of replies and one name kept coming up, Yvonne from her company 'Everything Ibiza'.

Lots of people expressed just how good she was. Genuine, professional and trustworthy. Just what I wanted.

I contacted her and explained our situation and she put me in touch with one of her employees, Karen. We engaged in a few bits of email dialogue explaining our likes, dislikes, budget, etc. We had said we were not too fussy where we were in Ibiza, as we were very familiar with the island having visited many times over the years, but would prefer not to look in the built up central Ibiza town areas.

Karen sent us several properties within our budget and we soon realised that we would have to go for an apartment. We would have loved to have had a detached house, but that was out of the question.

We even tentatively discussed selling our home in the UK and combining budgets, but living out there full time would have been a whole other ball game, plus a potential minefield with Brexit.

Over time, we looked forward to the photos, properties, and voice messages from Karen in her great cockney accent. I loved it! She was fantastic and always brightened our day!

Obviously COVID-19 put paid to any visits to Ibiza for quite a while. We were itching to get out there, but it was red and amber on the government traffic light system, and therefore travel was restricted. We had to bide our time, but still had great fun looking online.

After what seemed like ages, we finally got the green light to travel! We couldn't wait! Out of four properties we had earmarked as interesting, Lisa and I had already done a virtual tour of one with Karen via Facebook live.

It was a relatively exclusive complex of 12 apartments and the one we had seen was nicely appointed with three bedrooms, two bathrooms, and was fully furnished.

It ticked a lot of our boxes and was in a great area called Port des Torrent which was in the south west corner, five minutes from the beach, surrounded by amazing views and on two sides, countryside.

We couldn't wait to get there!

The other pretty major life changing event that was happening alongside all this, was that my business partner (also called Lisa, just to confuse things) and I, were aiming to sell our business, 'Personal Space'. We had reached just over 20 years together, which is quite impressive for any business, so I guess we must have been doing something right!

Despite some trepidation, 'business' Lisa (as I called her to others, to not mix her up with 'my' Lisa), explained that as the lease on our studio was coming up for renewal, she didn't want to continue. As soon as she said it, she was very emotional. I think she had been concerned about what my reaction would be.

In fact, it would work well for both of us. I had already had a conversation with my Lisa about winding down a bit, and possibly retiring early. So, a plan was hatched.

Business Lisa and I discussed whether we should just close or try and sell it as a going concern. We both agreed, after so much time and effort over the years, it would be great to see 'Personal Space' continue, plus we had to think of all our clients and the continuation of their training.

We both put some ideas down on paper, with the aim of attracting new owners. We had already discussed different avenues, and to approach some of the existing personal training studios in the area, but felt we needed to speak to the trainers who were already at our studio first, to see if they would be interested.

Well, one trainer, Nicole got back to us straight away and said that she and her boyfriend were definitely interested. Great!

After a full disclosure of earnings, costs, and what was to be included in the sale, we struck a deal. Business Lisa and I were extremely pleased that the 'Personal Space' name that we worked so hard to keep would live on.

The next few months were quite stressful. We had to do a lot of remedial work on our studio space following the landlord's dilapidation survey, whilst still training our lovely clients.

The gym was really taking shape, but it was hard balancing all the decorating, wall tanking, and tidying, getting it all ship shape and Bristol fashion!

I had spoken to my clients about what was happening, and I was a little nervous about how they might receive the news. Despite their obvious disappointment, I thought they took it quite well. I think they liked the fact that 'Personal Space' would continue, and that I could introduce them to their new trainer, and hand over my knowledge on their training schedules if required.

After many, many, hours of extra work on the studio, the time had come to do the handover. We knew the business was going to good hands, but there was a tinge of sadness was about letting go, but you know what they say - onwards and upwards!

Both Business Lisa and I had a celebratory meal on our final day together, with the obligatory selfie outside 'Personal Space' . Despite being quite different in our personalities, we had developed a great working relationship, and 'Personal Space' was a true success story.

You know what that say, as one door closes, another opens. With the promise of easier times, after what had been a turbulent personal life over the last few years, I was very much looking forward to opening a much easier door, into the next chapter.

The time had very nearly come to go to Ibiza to finally look at properties! Yay!

As we had already had two holidays to Ibiza cancelled over the last year or so, I had booked a special hotel, in Playa den Bossa to have as our base when looking.

After such a long wait, we had to pinch ourselves that we could finally fly, and more importantly find our dream holiday home. To comply with COVID-19 guidelines we had to complete a passenger locator form before we travelled and for our return. We needed to provide proof of double Covid vaccinations, complete a lateral flow test whilst in Ibiza, and a PCR test within the first few days of our return. We also had to wear masks for the whole travel process - in the airport, flying and the taxi transfer.

Quite a rigmarole, but worth it for the end result.

The whole journey went smoothly, and we couldn't wait to get to our room. Luckily a room was available straight away, despite the fact that we were a few hours early. We had the offer of a higher floor room to take later, or one a few floors down now, so we chose the latter, as it had been an early start and we couldn't wait to relax.

The room was great, and the bath, which had an awesome view over the beach, was also a spa bath, perfect to unwind our muscles.

I had already booked a rental car for visiting the four earmarked properties, so after we had a breakfast fit for royalty, we set off.

It took quite the effort to remember to keep to the right side of the road, but we got to the other side of the island without any hiccups. (Despite Lisa being a very nervous passenger).

We arrived a little early and waited for Karen outside the property. When she arrived, I really felt we'd known her for ages because we had Face Timed so often. We felt like friends already. She enthusiastically welcomed us, and we were introduced to Yvonne, the company owner.

She reminded me of my best friend Will, who lived in London for many years, because everyone was called 'mate'. It didn't matter who you were, you were always mate! It was familiar and friendly, and we felt at home straight away!

We looked around the first property and it was just like the pictures. It was very tastefully decorated, had a lovely roof terrace, a built in sunshade and artificial grass floor, together with lots of potted plants.

The lounge had a lovely 'Ibiza' *feel* to it, with a zebra print rug, wooden rush shades and nice ambient lighting. The kitchen was big and well equipped, and the bedrooms were all a good size. The only factor going against this one was the outside of the building, which was nothing to write home about. The complex was also big and felt quite impersonal. This one was a little over budget too, so it had to tick a lot (all?) of the boxes for us to proceed.

Yvonne left us at this point, as she had just wanted to say hello, so we knew who she was, and we went on to the second property with Karen.

This was the one we had already looked at via Facebook, and the one which, on paper, we were most keen on. As we entered the complex, we both felt good vibes even without saying anything to each other. This complex was smaller, and felt more exclusive. The gardens and communal pool were immaculate.

This apartment had three bedrooms and two bathrooms, so perfect for us, with a lovely airy lounge. We particularly liked the big, angled window high up in the roof which flooded natural light inwards. Once again, it was well appointed and came fully furnished, which was a big bonus.

We went up to the large roof terrace, and were very impressed with the amazing views of both countryside and sea. There was a big chimney BBQ and a sink with running water. Both Lisa and I wanted outdoor space and this terrace, whilst basic, had a lot of potential!

The apartment ticked a lot of boxes and was exactly how we thought it would be. We had a brief chat with one of the other apartment owners and he seemed really friendly. He gave us the 'skinny' on the complex and made me like it even more.

The third property was on the other side of the bay, in San Antonio. This one was interesting, as it was above the famous Cafe del Mar, on the sunset strip. I'd sat along that strip many a time over the years.

It was the place where people came to just watch the sun set, along with the DJ's playing chill-out tracks to suit the mood. When the sun finally set, the whole beach and all the people in restaurants and bars would clap in unison, it was an amazing experience. Next to that was the infamous Cafe Mambo where BBC Radio One holds their annual live weekends, and all of the world's best DJs play on the terrace.

We knew this place would be busy, (certainly not tranquil!), but the views totally sold the flat. When we entered, we were both drawn immediately to the small terrace with the amazing view, looking out across the bay. Little did we think, that after being down on the sunset strip countless times, we would be looking at a property above it all!

The flat did need some work which wouldn't have mattered, but I think it was nostalgia that endeared the flat to us. For me it didn't feel right, my gut instinct was kicking in again.

After this viewing, there was one flat to go, just across the bay from where we had been. This one had lots of natural light and lovely sea views, but it was quite a bit smaller. We could quickly see that it would be too small for us, and that it wouldn't work if we were all out there as a family. It was a shame, as the views were fantastic. We asked Karen to join us for a late lunch, and she recommended a restaurant not that far from where we were.

We reflected on the day's viewings and there was clearly one front runner - the one we'd already viewed in the complex of 12. Lisa and I discussed this for most of the rest of the day and night.

The next day we rang Karen and said we wanted to make an offer - how exciting!

We made a low-ish offer as the property was just a little over budget, so we waited with bated breath to see what the owner thought.

Well, he kept us waiting for quite a while because he wanted to respond after the annual complex meeting, which was just under a week away.

Lisa and I both felt that he wanted a higher offer, and our suspicions were confirmed. He wanted to only drop by 5,000 Euro from the full asking price, and said he was firm on this. Damn. That was too much. We couldn't stretch that far.

I think we both said that in that case we might wait until next year as there was no real rush. The rest of the holiday we tried to just forget about properties, and enjoy a well needed break away.

When we returned home, we had a voicemail from Karen.

"Alright mate? I thought you might be interested to

know there is a slightly smaller two bed just come up on the same complex that you liked. It's with another agent, but I can speak to them if you still want to go through me?"

"Ooh yes please Karen! Could you send over the details, and we will have a look!"

We were very excited because we loved the complex and thought we'd lost out. Amazing news!

We decided to organise another virtual showing, so we could at least get a good initial idea. Karen led the viewing, but the other estate agent chipped in with useful information. He also very kindly sent us a full video of the whole apartment, including the roof terrace.

The apartment was very similar to the other apartment we looked at, it just needed a bit of a tidy up, but that was just cosmetic - easy stuff and a nice little project. We were obviously down one bedroom, but we said that we could put a sofa bed in the lounge, if necessary.

Now, despite the fact we hadn't seen it in the flesh, we knew the complex and loved it. Lisa and I had no hesitation in putting an offer in. We told Karen and waited.

We didn't get an immediate response like they do in the TV property programmes. I always wondered if they time edited those?

Anyway, that evening after I had just popped upstairs, Karen rang. I missed it but called back.

The offer had been declined and they came back with a counter offer. After more deliberation, we decided to up it a bit and worry about finding the extra later.

Karen rang back after a little while, to tell us that the offer had been accepted, and we finally had our holiday home, including everything in it!

Yes!! At last!

After all that effort, the probate, house clearance and selling, we had finally realised a dream. Mum and Dad would be so pleased, it was a huge shame that they would never be able to enjoy it. We did feel they would be there with us in spirit.

What a journey it had been!

At times it felt like we weren't going to make it. So many twists, turns and issues, but we had made it, finally.

It was now time to look forward to calmer waters, and enjoy ourselves - I really did feel like we deserved it.

CHAPTER EIGHTEEN
WHAT I'VE LEARNT

I can certainly say I've learnt an awful lot about myself, life, and people, going through the whole process of dealing with Mum and Dad's lives.

I know there are many families out there that have been affected by Alzheimer's and dementia. Sadly, my story is one of many, but I do think it's unusual for both parents to be affected, hence the book.

I always said I wanted to write about the experience because I want to help others understand, and hopefully learn something from what we went through as a family. If you have learnt a few things, or if I've made you think differently about the issues raised, then I'll have done what I set out to do.

I wasn't too sure when I started writing how it was going to go, or how easy the process would be. Despite the very emotional subject, and stirring up some of those feelings within me again, it's been a very worthwhile process and I would also now say, cathartic in nature.

I'm so pleased the story is out. Even if it's just a record for my close family to know and understand what happened, but I hope it attracts a wider audience.

Sadly, my twins, Tom and Liv, do not remember a huge amount about my parents, as they were so very young, and they didn't see Mum much in the later stages of her illness and life, because they had already said their goodbyes.

My eldest two, Josie and Ella, do remember quite a lot, as they used to go and stay over with my mum and dad when Lisa and I went out. They can remember doing lots of making and baking, as Mum loved getting them involved in the kitchen. Scones, cheese straws, cupcakes, etc. Ella especially liked any excuse to get her hands messy!

They can remember playing at Spider Cottage, dressing up, and playing in their bedroom. Also watching their favourite TV programmes like 'Rosie and Jim' and 'Teletubbies'.

There was even one time Mum put on the film Gremlins (VHS cassette to give you the era!), thinking it was all about the sweet Mogwai on the cover, but then soon realised that there were a few monsters in it. (I think they had a few nightmares after that one!).

Both my mum and dad loved all their grandchildren

immeasurably. I just hope they felt and remember that.

It was interesting to see how those around you - friends and family - deal with the shock of a diagnosis like Mum's and Dad's. Firstly, there can be level of denial from those closest; disbelief that this can really be happening to their loved one.

It can be hard to know at which specific moment the Alzheimer's or dementia starts to have an effect, and at what point action is required. As we age, there is a natural decline in some cognitive function anyway, but it's noticing the bigger picture, and putting two and two together.

There is a grey area of degradation, that's not clear or linear by any means, and it appears that whilst there are commonalities, each person diagnosed can have a very different journey or pathway.

If I think back to both Mum's and Dad's lives, they had many friends and an active social life, but that waned significantly towards the end. Yes, of course, Mum wasn't able to engage, but I think Dad, struggling with the enormity of it all, stopped communicating with people.

Dad didn't tell everyone what was going on, and those that did know were ringing me to check that everything was ok, as they'd left messages and written, but to no avail.

The other side of the coin was that some friends found it very difficult to deal with. I've had family friends say that they didn't like watching or experiencing Mum's decline. It did surprise me how few of Mum and Dad's friends visited in the later years. There could be many reasons for that, but either way it was sad.

Mum pre-Alzheimer's, was a huge contrast to the person she was becoming, and had become.

Closer family members knew that something wasn't quite right. My nan, if you remember, had expressed concern after Mum had stayed with her. My mum's brothers and their wives, after Dad's procrastination, had said that something had to be done because they noticed Mum's personality and demeanour changing. I wonder if her outer circle had noticed certain things but brushed it off?

Without a doubt, those with Alzheimer's or dementia have a huge impact on all of those around them. In my case, Mum's mental and physical decline, and that of my dad had significant impacts on close family, especially Lisa and I.

The rollercoaster I frequently refer to throughout this book, references the huge ups and downs of both Mum's and Dad's journeys. Periods of calm, the steadier, flatter tracks, and then big peaks and troughs, representing the 'firefighting' and crisis management needed. There were a few tight twists and G-force turns as new issues reared their heads, all adding to the journey as a whole.

Whilst I've said that one coping strategy is to tackle one day at a time, (and that holds true), conversely, I'm also really hoping that the issues raised, throughout the book, encourage you to think ahead, to either avert or at least minimise any future issues and reduce the high peaks and low troughs of the rollercoaster.

One factor was not knowing Mum's true wishes for the future.

A very tough conversation for anyone to have, but I think if you know, you can follow through with exact wishes, knowing you are doing the best to abide by them.

Obviously, we knew Mum very well, but we were still guessing on her final wishes and what, if anything she wanted throughout her care.

Initially, I didn't understand much about Alzheimer's or dementia, but it's good to remember there is help out there - financial, educational, institutional, local and national, support networks, singing for the brain groups, main carer support, and not to mention the carers that came to Mum and Dad's home.

The home visit carers increased the time that my mum was able to stay at home and helped my dad to fulfil his wish for longer than would have been possible alone.

We could not have functioned as effectively without

their visits, initially once, and then three times a day. They were our eyes and ears and made us all feel safer that someone was checking in with them regularly.

I can't praise the healthcare teams enough. They all do such an amazing job, both the ones that visited Mum and Dad's house and the ones at Holywell Nursing Home.

Depending on your financial status there are different types of help to assist within care. At the time of writing, legislation is being discussed to ensure people don't have to lose all of their savings or house, to pay for their care.

We were very lucky with Mum's care home – Holywell - they were amazing.

She'd been there for her respite care, and they knew her, which really helped her transition, but I know sometimes people just don't have a choice as to where they end up.

Over the earlier years Mum went to several homes for respite care and in my opinion, most were very good, with amazing staff. They do however vary in their ability to offer time to residents, and the budget to offer additional activities, entertainment, or just things to pass the time. I had heard of animals being brought into the home, also singers and fun games. At the first respite home Mum was in, one lady was even given a 'dolly' to look after. She really thought it was real, and cared for it like her own child.

We were extremely lucky to have such supportive family and friends around us, the help was immeasurable.

Trying to run my business which demanded very long hours, early am to late pm, together with doing family stuff with the kids, whilst at the same time ensuring Mum and Dad were safe, and not in any danger made things more complicated.

The guilt trip kicked in often, and constant 'self-talk' about whether I should adjust my working hours, to allow more time for Mum and Dad. It was often like balancing on a knife edge trying to devote the right amount of time and focus to work, family and care.

Thinking back, I was always stressed and worried about them, but I also worried about making enough money to pay the bills. Lisa and I, when the kids were small, did struggle financially, and I certainly didn't want to be in that situation again. Four kids, a mortgage, and both self-employed creates a sense of jeopardy!

One extremely important task is to get the power of attorney (POA) sorted well ahead of time, and I would say to include more than one trustworthy person.

It can still be applied for when the person in question is compos mentis, because it's a shared responsibility, and doesn't mean the person with the POA should take sole charge until the subject of the POA needs them to.

Based on the paperwork trail nightmare that we had, I'd also check that wills are up to date, together with all the legal paperwork, and that it can all be found easily. This includes solicitor's details, house deeds, bank details and utilities, etc.

On reflection, I think Lisa and I did well, which is a good feeling. I was always told to remember the 80/20 rule - if you are getting it right 80% of the time then you are doing a bloody good job!

I've learnt you can always improve no matter what, and to celebrate the little successes. Try not to aim for perfection, it's overrated!!

The memory clinic was the glue between myself, Dad and the doctors, who were very proactive in assisting with his care plan. The group meetings also offered a lifeline for those loved ones taking on the caring role.

Without a doubt, Lisa, my wife, was my absolute rock. She helped, supported, and managed to keep me (semi) sane. It was hugely important for me to have someone with whom to talk through any issues and just know someone had your back.

I couldn't have done it without her.

As you have hopefully gathered from my musings, I loved

both my parents dearly, so it was hugely important to me to ensure they received the best care and were safe at all times. This followed through right to their funerals and their headstone.

If I'm being honest, I was probably closest to my Mum, but that's partly because of how she was. I had more of an affinity with her personality and her warmness. Dad was just harder to get to, but I still loved him dearly.

Don't get me wrong he had a very gentle, and calm nature, but was much more reserved, and tended to have a bit of a barrier up. He struggled to show or share his emotions, it was his protective coat of armour from his childhood. He kept his emotions close to his chest, which as I said before often infuriated Mum. Bless him, that was just his way.

He once told me there were two people he had most respected in his lifetime, namely, myself and his own father. I think that was his way of saying he loved me. I was told by others that he was proud of me.

It's because of this that I make sure all my kids know that I love them very much. They know because I tell them!

It was very important for me to get the funerals right for each of them and to ensure the headstone fully encapsulated and signified who they were and what they stood for. Hence the inclusion of the photograph of them both together on the headstone.

As you get older, you appreciate life more than you did as a youngster, especially having gone through the trauma of my parents' lives in the later years. I'm a firm believer that life always has lessons for you, and whilst I greatly enjoy the nicer lessons, the ones that kick you up the butt, often give a deeper level of learning.

I can honestly say I've learnt more from my harder lessons about myself and life, than the easier ones.

The process of writing my story has helped me realise that despite all the 'firefighting', trouble-shooting and terrible lows, I got through it to become a stronger person. I am mentally stronger, having learnt an awful lot along the way, and it all went pretty well, everything considered.

I know this experience has made me appreciate life more, and as a consequence I'm grateful. Grateful for life and for living. As the saying goes, 'Life's too short', and when you see what both my parents had to deal with, then you try to make the best of every day and every moment.

I have always kept an eye on my health and wellness, but as I'm getting older, I'm using scientific research to increase and prolong it.

I've always trained throughout my life with both cardiovascular exercise and resistance training, and both have a place in fitness. Rather than leave things to chance, I also get my bloods checked to monitor relevant markers, and I've been working with a nutritionist to assist in maximising overall health.

It certainly has crossed my mind that both parents suffering with Alzheimer's and dementia, could increase my chances of getting it.

I decided I would do as much as I could do lower that risk. Lifestyle factors, it appears, can make a difference, despite genetic predisposition. At the time of writing, lifestyle factors are more likely to affect the prospect of developing dementia than genetics.

Time will tell.

I'm not sure I would change too much in the way that our journey unfolded, when you consider the enormity of the task. As Shrek said to Donkey in the film, "…that'll do Donkey, that'll do."

Yes, if I tried hard, I'm sure I could berate myself, but what good would that do?

At some point you have to make peace with yourself and find comfort, so that's what I've done. All things considered, I think I did well, and that's important to move onwards from a very tough period of my life.

I often think about Dad, on learning of his dementia

diagnosis. Having cared for Mum for many years I feel sure, although he never said it, he must have thought, 'Is what happened to Di, going to happen to me?'

It certainly crossed my mind.

In comparison to Mum, Dad's dementia effects, apart from towards the end, were quite a bit milder.

Did the accident, and falling out of bed, then contracting Sepsis save him from the ever so slow decline that afflicted her?

Obviously, I wanted him to live, but after speaking to the specialist at the hospital, where Dad sadly passed away, it was clear he was giving up.

He was lying in bed, not washing or shaving, despite encouragement, not watching television, or even reading, which was definitely his default mode.

I wholeheartedly believe that the early years of looking after Mum had massive implications for his overall wellness in his later years, but also he wasn't the best at looking after himself.

Mum had always taken care of him – ensuring he ate well and did the things he enjoyed. When she was no longer there to do that for him, he wasn't able to do it for himself.

I tried to fill Mum's shoes when we ordered online food or went food shopping, but it was an uphill battle.

Wiltshire Farm Foods helped get some better nutrition in him (and Mum) and it certainly made it easier to prepare for mealtime. It's little things like this that, which made the day-to-day a little less stressful.

He did incredibly well with Mum. That Christmas they stayed with us made me realise very quickly exactly what he was having to do to look after Mum.

I always remember him saying, and he repeated it to me many times, that he missed the 'off the cuff' comments from Mum, like "…ooh, look at that", or "What do you think of this?" Or even a simple question with an expected reply, but instead there was nothing.

This sadness obviously paled into insignificance when the time came that Mum had no clue who you were. I felt so much for Dad when his own wife didn't recognise him, that must have been incredibly tough. It was tough for me too, but I dealt with it by still acting as if she did, and hoped there might be a little sliver of recognition somewhere, at sometime.

That's the thing, you don't always know how much the person with Alzheimer's or dementia understands, so it's best to still do things the same, just in case something is getting through.

It was important to consider all the senses: auditory, smell, taste, touch and sight, even more so in the later stages, hence the lights, the flowers, the diffuser, the facials, the brushing hair, the holding hands, etc.

I needed to feel I was doing my best whatever the circumstances.

Whilst Mum going into a care home was against my dad's wishes, the choice was taken out of his hands. Whilst this was a tough call, at least he did not have to make it. In some way, it was made easier because it had to happen for Mum to get the level of care she needed.

He found it difficult going to see her, as did I, but we went because we loved her, cared for her and wanted the best for her.

Despite how lovely all the staff at the care home were, it still must have been very frightening and confusing for Mum at times.

So here is another important learning, the importance of looking after yourself whilst caring for others. It is quite easy to forget about your own health and wellbeing when you are so focused on others. In fact, it's critical for the patient's health, that you stay in optimal health too. Easier said than done, but I think at least if you are aware of it, it helps.

I also believe it's important to remember the person all the way through their life. The condition, whilst catastrophic, does not define that person's whole life.

Remember all the good times. Use the photographs and videos to remind you. I think because Mum's condition had gone on for so long, I had actually forgotten a big part of the real Mum.

Dad, apart from towards the end with his depression and the affects of the dementia, was still mostly as I knew him. He did not go too far down the same road as Mum.

It is sad sometimes to look at the photographs and see what was, but it also keeps the memories alive and can bring great joy to remember all those good times.

I haven't played the aforementioned videos that show Mum and Dad at various stages through their life at the time of writing this. I think I will have to be in the right frame of mind for those, but I will be getting all those slides put into a digital format, so we can play them on the television.

If you've got this far, then I truly thank you for reading my story. Whatever your reasons for picking up the book, I hope it has managed to help, or at least make you understand, in some way.

If you are currently dealing with any of the issues raised in this book, I sincerely wish you strength to deal with your own personal journey, whatever that might be. Know that you will be stronger by going through it.

Be kind to yourself and have a personal care plan to maximise your own health and wellness, as it's easy to put yourself last in the pecking order. Consider movement and exercise, feeding the body with good nutrition, keeping the brain working, getting good quality sleep, engaging with friends and sharing concerns with those around you and professionals if need be.

I hope your rollercoaster is a low ranking one, with minimal twists, turns, peaks and troughs. That you become an expert at 'firefighting', by thinking ahead of what some of the issues might be, unless of course, you just need to focus on one day at a time.

USEFUL CONTACTS

ALZHEIMERS SOCIETY

Address: 43-44 Crutched Friars, London, EC3N2AE

Tel: 0330 333 0804

Email: Enquiries@alzheimers.org.uk

Website: alzheimers.org.uk

Connect support line: 0330 150 3456

They give access and details into what local support is available for you, by putting in your details. They can give you specifics on activities and support groups, care in the home, and in care you own home, day care, any further information you might need, and getting help with transport.

Useful resource and support network for getting help and understanding.

They provide guidance on what to do from a carer and patient perspective.

ALZHEIMERS ASSOCIATION

Website: alz.org

An American site but some useful information and educational resources.

This association offer a variety of in person and virtual events and offer a resource for local community help and support. They have a 24 hour helpline. They offer a connected living site where you can share your experiences with others having a similar diagnosis.

They offer peer or professional led groups for caregivers, free online educational programmes. They have up to date research information which you can read. There is a live chat option.

AGE UK

Address: 7th floor, One America Square, 17 Crosswall, London, EC3N2LB

Tel: 0800 169 80 80

Advice line: 0800 055 6112 (8am-7pm)

Email: contact@ageuk.org.uk

Website: ageuk.org.uk

They provide details on memory cafes, creative workshops, specialist support groups, & cognitive stimulation therapy programmes both remotely, and face to face.

NEXT STEPS

Website: nextsteps.org.uk

Next Steps helps you to find the right support, whilst you are waiting for your memory assessment. It covers what to expect, how to sustain your well- being, where to go for support, whether it be emotional, clinical, social or practical. There is a contact form on their website.

DEMENTIA UK

Address: 7th floor, One Aldgate, London, EC3N 1RE
Tel: 020 8036 5400
Email: info@dementiauk.org
Website: dementiauk.org
Helpline: 0800 888 6678

Useful organisation for Dementia information, learning types of Dementia, including early onset. It also provides information on support networks and services. There is also helpline to call.

NHS

Website: nhs.uk

Offer a guide to help learn and understand about all Dementias, what help and support is available, care homes, money, legal affairs, assessment, symptoms and diagnosis.

ALARM PENDANTS AND TELECARE

SERVICES

Email: which.co.uk

Customer serve call centre: 02922670000

I would heartily encourage the use of alarm safety pendants, if you are concerned with any loved ones being at risk of falling. There are a number of companies that offer the service.

When researching I found that Which, the independent review company, had compiled a review of telecare services and providers.

WILTSHIRE FARM FOODS

Website: wiltshirefarmfoods.com

They provided easy nutritious meals for both my parents that were delivered to their house. They included meals at different stages of preparation and consistency to minimise choking. There are other companies available but they liked & used these specifically.

UK CARE GUIDE

Website: ukcareguide.co.uk

A one stop site that offers many things including

equipment to help around the home, including aids to assist mobility, technology, etc. It also explains about financial, legal, care, and well-being matters.

FINDING A SOLICITOR

Website: solicitors.lawsociety.org.uk

Support centre: 020 7320 5650

There is also an independent regulated solicitors register;

Website: sra.org.uk

I was lucky enough to find a local solicitor who was able to sort all of my legal work necessary. She dealt with the house sale, probate, power of attorney etc, which made it a lot easier being all in one place. She took a lot of heat off me, and saved hours or work and a huge amount of stress by taking it of my hands. I found a database of solicitors which might help you find someone if you haven't had a personal recommendation.

CITIZENS ADVICE BUREAU

Website: citizensadvice.org.uk

There is a search bar where you put in your postcode to find the nearest centre here also.

Advice line (England): 0800 144 8848

I think these would be a good resource to find out what's

needed to manage someone's affairs, what allowances you might get as a carer, and any specifics relating to benefits available, money matters, law, & health.

WILL MAKING

Website: moneysavingexpert.com/family/free-cheap-wills/

Despite Martin Lewis selling this, it still provides trusted information. It seems that not all will writers are regulated. I would heartily encourage to get a will made up or updated if you haven't already. Obviously with the problems we had in my parents case, we wanted to make it easier for our own children. I found this guide which helps to explain the pitfalls;

FINDING A CARE HOME

Website: lottie.org
Phone: 0330 912 8126

When I was looking locally for respite for Dad I already knew where to look just by local recommendation, however I found this national database that has had good reviews on Trustpilot.

You can search for residential, Dementia, nursing and

respite homes under different regions.

TRUSTPILOT

Website: uk.trustpilot.com

A useful site that has real world reviews of many companies and services. It's always useful to get real feedback from others as opposed to manufactured or paid promotion. Use it to double check or educate yourself on any business's that you might want to deal with.

SOCIAL MEDIA AND YOUTUBE

There is a huge amount of research and material about Dementia, Alzheimer's and brain health. It can get quite confusing with either mis -information or not being as accessible, being aimed at the medical or the research community.

I found a Dr couple on Instagram who are very clued up and explain quite technical subjects in more layperson terms. They have lots of reading material in the form of books, and listening podcasts, vlog regularly, are on YouTube, and have an online community to discuss issues.

Look for: thebraindocs

Names: Drs Ayesha and Dean Sherzai

I hope this goes some way in offering some support and help in your journey, my thoughts will be with you. I will include my personal details, should you want to get in touch for any reason. All the very best, Stuart.

Stuartdollery121@gmail.com

Printed in Great Britain
by Amazon